Autodesk® Inventor® 2018
Design Tools and Strategies

Student Guide
Mixed Units - 1ˢᵗ Edition

ASCENT - Center for Technical Knowledge®
Autodesk® Inventor® 2018
Design Tools and Strategies
Mixed Units - 1st Edition

Prepared and produced by:

ASCENT Center for Technical Knowledge
630 Peter Jefferson Parkway, Suite 175
Charlottesville, VA 22911

866-527-2368
www.ASCENTed.com

Lead Contributor: Jennifer MacMillan

ASCENT - Center for Technical Knowledge is a division of Rand Worldwide, Inc., providing custom developed knowledge products and services for leading engineering software applications. ASCENT is focused on specializing in the creation of education programs that incorporate the best of classroom learning and technology-based training offerings.

We welcome any comments you may have regarding this student guide, or any of our products. To contact us please email: feedback@ASCENTed.com.

Contents

Preface

The *Autodesk® Inventor® 2018: Design Tools and Strategies* student guide provides instruction on how to incorporate the use of top-down design and advanced modeling techniques into your design environment.

This student guide begins with an introduction to top-down design and the Autodesk® Inventor® software tools that can be used. There is a focus on multi-body design, deriving components, working with layouts and sketch blocks, and how associative links and adaptive parts can help you incorporate design intent into your models so they react as expected to change.

This student guide also includes chapters that cover Generative Shape Design, Frame Generator, and Design Accelerator, teaching you how you can use these advanced design tools to quickly create designs that meet your requirements.

The topics covered in this student guide are also covered in the following ASCENT student guides, which include a broader range of advanced topics:
- *Autodesk® Inventor® 2018: Advanced Assembly Modeling*
- *Autodesk® Inventor® 2018: Advanced Part Modeling*

Objectives

- Define and compare the differences between bottom-up and top-down design.
- Learn how to enforce design intent using three major top-down design techniques.
- Create solid bodies and correctly assign features to specific solid bodies.
- Modify solid bodies in a model by moving, removing, splitting, combining, or redefining them.
- Create new parts and assemblies from the multi-bodies in a single part.
- Derive new geometry in a part by importing and referencing objects from a source part.
- Create and modify layouts and sketch blocks.
- Define and test the kinematic motion of an assembly with the use of nested sketch blocks.

- Create 3D models from sketch blocks.
- Break the associative link between a sketched feature and reference geometry.
- Specify geometric entities of part features to change, while controlling the size or location of other entities in an assembly.
- Create a Shape Generator study that sets a goal to meet a mass reduction target.
- Assign criteria in a Shape Generator study to accurately define a model's working environment.
- Promote a Shape Generator study to the modeling environment.
- Quickly and easily create structural frames and defining the location of structural frame members using a skeletal wireframe part.
- Adjust frame member ends to obtain required joints.
- Create and publish custom frame member profiles to the Content Center.
- Automatically create geometry using component generators.

Note on Software Setup

This student guide assumes a standard installation of the software using the default preferences during installation. Lectures and practices use the standard software templates and default options for the Content Libraries.

Students and Educators can Access Free Autodesk Software and Resources

Autodesk challenges you to get started with free educational licenses for professional software and creativity apps used by millions of architects, engineers, designers, and hobbyists today. Bring Autodesk software into your classroom, studio, or workshop to learn, teach, and explore real-world design challenges the way professionals do.

Get started today - register at the Autodesk Education Community and download one of the many Autodesk software applications available.

Visit www.autodesk.com/joinedu/

Note: Free products are subject to the terms and conditions of the end-user license and services agreement that accompanies the software. The software is for personal use for education purposes and is not intended for classroom or lab use.

Lead Contributor: Jennifer MacMillan

With a dedication for engineering and education, Jennifer has spent over 20 years at ASCENT managing courseware development for various CAD products. Trained in Instructional Design, Jennifer uses her skills to develop instructor-led and web-based training products as well as knowledge profiling tools.

Jennifer has achieved the Autodesk Certified Professional certification for Inventor and is also recognized as an Autodesk Certified Instructor (ACI). She enjoys teaching the training courses that she authors and is also very skilled in providing technical support to end-users.

Jennifer holds a Bachelor of Engineering Degree as well as a Bachelor of Science in Mathematics from Dalhousie University, Nova Scotia, Canada.

Jennifer MacMillan has been the Lead Contributor for *Autodesk Inventor: Design Tools and Strategies* since its initial release in 2017.

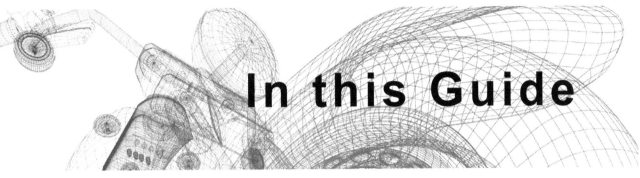

In this Guide

The following images highlight some of the features that can be found in this Student Guide.

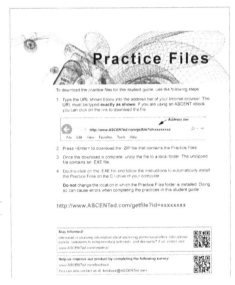

FTP link for practice files

Practice Files

The Practice Files page tells you how to download and install the practice files that are provided with this student guide.

Learning Objectives for the chapter

Chapters

Each chapter begins with a brief introduction and a list of the chapter's Learning Objectives.

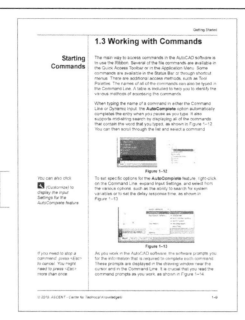

Instructional Content

Each chapter is split into a series of sections of instructional content on specific topics. These lectures include the descriptions, step-by-step procedures, figures, hints, and information you need to achieve the chapter's Learning Objectives.

Side notes

Side notes are hints or additional information for the current topic.

Practice Objectives

Practices

Practices enable you to use the software to perform a hands-on review of a topic.

Some practices require you to use prepared practice files, which can be downloaded from the link found on the Practice Files page.

Chapter Review Questions

Chapter review questions, located at the end of each chapter, enable you to review the key concepts and learning objectives of the chapter.

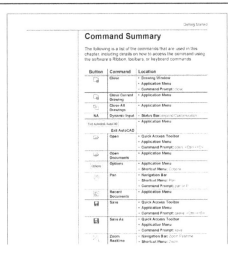

Command Summary

The Command Summary is located at the end of each chapter. It contains a list of the software commands that are used throughout the chapter, and provides information on where the command is found in the software.

Icons in this Student Guide

The following icons are used to help you quickly and easily find helpful information.

New in **2018** — Indicates items that are new in the Autodesk Inventor 2018 software.

Enhanced in **2018** — Indicates items that have been enhanced in the Autodesk Inventor 2018 software.

Practice Files

To download the practice files for this student guide, use the following steps:

1. Type the URL shown below into the address bar of your Internet browser. The URL must be typed **exactly as shown**. If you are using an ASCENT ebook, you can click on the link to download the file.

Address bar

http://www.ascented.com/getfile?id=corrumpo

File   Edit   View   Favorites   Tools   Help

2. Press <Enter> to download the .ZIP file that contains the Practice Files.

3. Once the download is complete, unzip the file to a local folder. The unzipped file contains an .EXE file.

4. Double-click on the .EXE file and follow the instructions to automatically install the Practice Files on the C:\ drive of your computer.

   Do not change the location in which the Practice Files folder is installed. Doing so can cause errors when completing the practices in this student guide.

http://www.ascented.com/getfile?id=corrumpo

Stay Informed!
Interested in receiving information about upcoming promotional offers, educational events, invitations to complimentary webcasts, and discounts? If so, please visit:
www.ASCENTed.com/updates/

Help us improve our product by completing the following survey:
www.ASCENTed.com/feedback
You can also contact us at: *feedback@ASCENTed.com*

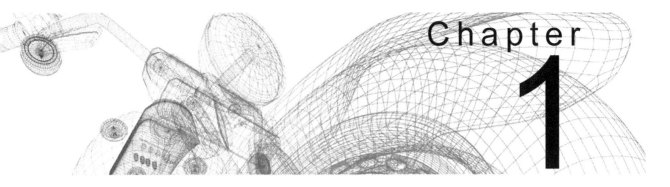

Introduction to Top-Down Design

The top-down design approach places critical information in a top-level assembly, then communicates that information to lower levels of the product structure. Planning the assembly using the top-down design approach helps create clean, reusable geometry that interacts as expected with the rest of the assembly.

Learning Objectives in this Chapter

- Define and compare the differences between bottom-up and top-down design.
- Describe how to enforce design intent using three major top-down design techniques.
- Describe the tools you would use to create 3D models from either sketch blocks generated in a layout sketch, multiple bodies in a single part, or a reference file.

1.1 Top-Down Design Process

Two different design methodologies can be used to build the top-level assembly: bottom-up and top-down.

Bottom-Up vs. Top Down Design

In a traditional bottom-up design approach, part geometry is created independently of the assembly and other components. Any design criteria established before modeling the part is not shared between models. Once all part models are completed, they are brought together for the first time in the assembly. At this point in the design, problems often result with the assembly because engineering information is not correctly communicated. Problems might include interference, misalignment, or incomplete design. Additionally, any modifications must be manually propagated throughout the assembly. The concept of bottom-up design is shown in Figure 1–1.

Figure 1–1

The top-down design approach places critical information in a top-level assembly, then communicates that information to lower levels of the product structure. The first step in creating a top-down design model is to create an initial assembly structure in the form of a reference part model. Design information is placed in a reference model using parametric design intent, solid bodies, sketch blocks, or other standard modeling tools. Lower level components and the assembly itself is then created manually or automatically depending on the design method.

Using the various Autodesk® Inventor® software techniques, you can create geometry referencing the initial reference model or other components in the assembly. Any changes made to the initial design intent is automatically propagated to all affected components.

The three main methods of top-down design, Layout Design, Adaptive Design, and Multi-Body Design, are shown in Figure 1–2.

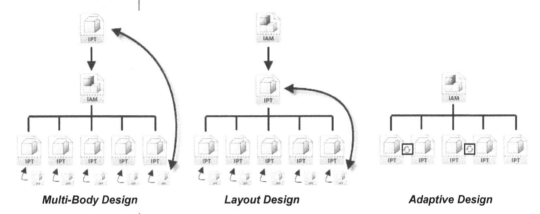

Multi-Body Design   **Layout Design**   **Adaptive Design**

Figure 1–2

Top-Down Design Process

Top-down design has been an engineering CAD methodology used in the Autodesk Inventor software for some time, where you create single part files (skeletons) in the context of an assembly model and use the part file to derive components for the assembly. Top-down design has been made easier with the use of tools that enable multi-body part files and layout designs. You can also use Adaptive reference modeling to implement a top-down design strategy in your assemblies.

As with any technique, using top-down design in your assemblies should involve a process. This process should be followed regardless of the technique (Multi-Body Modeling, Layout Design, or Adaptive Modeling) that you are using. Consider the following stages in the process:

1. **PLANNING** the assembly using top-down design helps create clean, reusable geometry that reacts as expected.
2. **ENFORCING** design intent ensures interactions and dependencies between components.
3. **CHANGING** top-level information propagates to all referenced components.

Planning

The top-down design technique organizes and helps enforce the interactions and dependencies between components. Many interactions and dependencies exist in an actual assembly and it is desirable to capture these dependencies when modeling. With appropriate planning during the initial design stage, you can consider all areas of a final model before creating any geometry.

Consider the following questions during the planning stage:

- What does the assembly do?

- How does a specific model interface with other components?

- What are the inputs and outputs of the assembly?

The answers to these questions help you to plan and correctly execute your design intent. Spending time planning the assembly helps you create a final model that reacts as expected.

Enforcing

Many commands and tools in the software can be used to enforce top-down design. The following are the three major top-down design techniques used to enforce design intent:

- Multi-Body Modeling

- Layout Design

- Adaptive Modeling

Multi-Body Modeling

Multi-Body part files enable you to create your entire assembly design in the Part environment using part modeling feature commands. The design is arranged into separate bodies in the single part file. Figure 1–3 shows a model that has two solid bodies. **Solid2** is selected and highlighted on the model. These separate bodies can then be extracted to derive individual parts for a new assembly.

Features can be shared between different bodies.

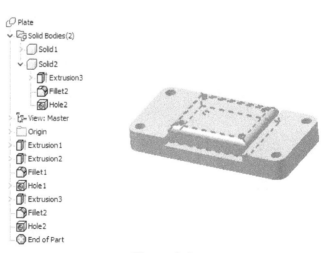

Figure 1–3

The advantages of using Multi-Body design include the following:

- Top-down design is more streamlined. You do not need to set up an initial complex file and directory structure to design parts in the context of a top-level assembly. The entire design resides in a single file. Bodies are later extracted to create parts.

- A complex part file can be better organized using separate bodies with respect to their function or position in the model.

- Relationships between bodies can be easily set up and broken.

- You can control the visibility of bodies as a group rather than at the individual feature level.

- This method is useful for plastic part design, where interior components for a predefined shape can be designed in context and then extracted.

Layout Design

To accomplish a top-down design environment using Layout Design, you convey the design intent of a model by using a 2D sketch as a central repository for overall dimensions, spatial locations, and the general shape of components. The design information is stored in the form of Sketch Blocks in the layout. An example of a 2D sketch (made up of multiple Sketch Blocks) is shown on the left in Figure 1–4. 3D models are generated based on the sketch, as shown on the right in Figure 1–4.

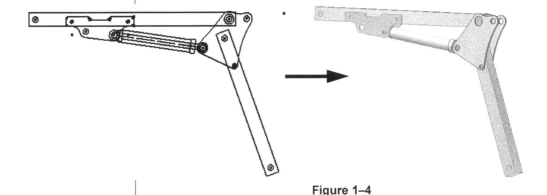

Figure 1–4

Layout Design is used for a number of reasons, including the following:

- **3D Geometry Creation:** The entities that are created in a layout sketch are used in a target model to derive the solid geometry, as shown in Figure 1–5. By doing this, you maintain a link to the layout sketch and any changes to the layout are propagated to the components.

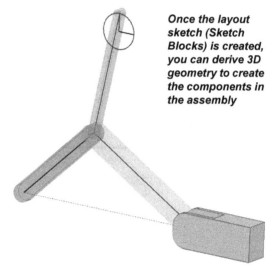

Once the layout sketch (Sketch Blocks) is created, you can derive 3D geometry to create the components in the assembly

Figure 1–5

- **Testing Assembly Motion:** When creating a layout sketch, the ability to test the motion of the assembly before spending time creating 3D geometry is a valuable asset. By modifying the sketch dimensions, as shown in Figure 1–6, you can ensure that you capture the required design intent before moving on with the design.

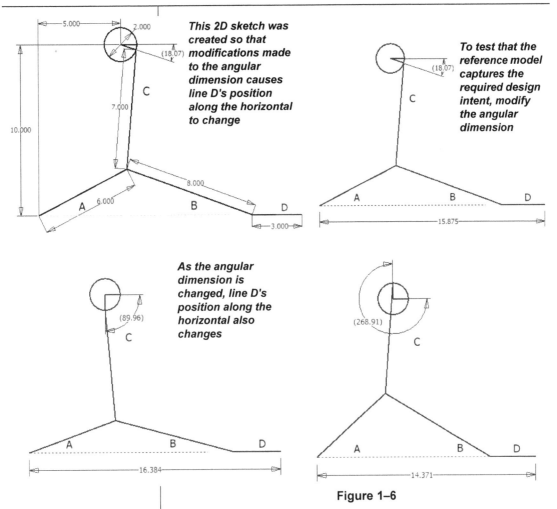

This 2D sketch was created so that modifications made to the angular dimension causes line D's position along the horizontal to change

To test that the reference model captures the required design intent, modify the angular dimension

As the angular dimension is changed, line D's position along the horizontal also changes

Figure 1–6

- **Controlling Parent/Child Relationships:** Deriving portions of geometry from a layout instead of referencing other components directly in an assembly reduces the chance of creating unwanted parent/child relationships between components. Using this technique makes operations (such as suppressing, deleting, and interchanging components) in the assembly easier, since fewer dependency relationships exist.

Adaptive Modeling

Adaptive Modeling, sometimes referred to as cross-part projection, uses references already inside the assembly for geometry creation by projecting references from one part to another. Typically, new parts are created directly inside the assembly to accomplish this, but can also be made to adapt even after assembly creation. Adaptive modeling has certain restrictions because of the nature of file associations and multiple occurrences of the same part inside an assembly.

Adaptive models are used for numerous reasons, including the following:

- **Creating Mating Parts:** You can adapt outlines of the geometry of parts to create a matching insert or outline, thus recreating the original geometry in a mating fashion. Updates to originating geometry update the references used on the new part. This is similar to using Project Geometry in a part file, but in this case, it is used to project geometry from other sources.

- **Determining Tolerances:** Use projected geometry to determine a reference of component placement or sizing inside a component that has to maintain a specific tolerance to the mating component. You can adjust the size of the original part and use parametric control in the new component to maintain the correct tolerance sizing.

- **Location of Geometry:** Use adaptive models with unconstrained sketches and features to enable the geometry to flex inside the assembly based on what is constrained. This permits for open design decisions during conceptual modeling or fit iterations.

Changing

By effectively planning for the required design intent and enforcing it using top-down design techniques, you can create an assembly model that reacts as expected when changes are made. You can make changes to the assembly by editing the reference model and then updating all components that reference it. By this stage in the design, all 3D models should be completed, enabling you to check fits, clearances, or interferences in the assembly. This enables you to quickly vary the design and functionality of the assembly.

1.2 Top-Down Design Tools

The following top-down design tools are discussed in more detail throughout this student guide.

Multi-Body Design Tools

Much like modeling a single body model, multi-bodies are modeled using the same feature commands to define different components in the assembly. The only difference is that each new feature is assigned to a body. Once multiple solid bodies exist in the model, you can further manipulate them. You can redefine them as part of another solid body, move them, split them, combine them, insert additional bodies from other models, or use them to create separate parts and assemblies.

Make Layout

Layouts are created and added as a grounded component in an assembly using the **Make Layout** command. A new standard part file is generated to hold the layout sketch that holds all of the design data. Once the sketch layout is created, you group the entities into sketch blocks to represent the components or subassemblies of the assembly.

Make Components & Make Part

Using the **Make Components** and **Make Part** commands, you can quickly create 3D models from the Layout design's sketch blocks or the bodies in a Multi-body Design. These components remain associative to their source, so that when changes are made to 2D sketch blocks or multi-bodied design, the generated 3D models also update.

Derive

Without the Layout Design and Multi-Body workflows, the manual methodology of using the **Derive** command with a reference model was tedious, but effective. This was commonly called Skeletal Modeling.

As a basis, deriving geometry is accomplished by accessing a reference model for data in order to create geometry in a new model. You can make changes to the assembly by editing the reference model and then updating all components that reference it.

Parts in Assembly

The Autodesk Inventor software enables you to create parts within the context of an assembly. As with assembly features, you need to be careful about creating feature relationships when creating a part in the assembly environment.

Assembly Features

Features can also be created in the top-level assembly or at the subassembly level. This process is often used to add secondary machining operations for weldments, but it can also be used to create alignment holes and other features. The important rules to remember with this tool are:

- It occurs at the assembly level and does not propagate geometry to the part level.

- Reference selection creates feature relationships.

Associative Links & Adaptive Parts

*Using **Copy Object** at the part level inside an assembly also can create associative links.*

Each time you reference geometry (i.e., projecting geometry, dimensioning to edges or faces on other components) to create a section of the sketched feature, the software applies an associative link between the reference geometry and the sketched feature. Associative links make the geometry *adaptive*.

Associative links are a powerful tool in design projects. Many dimensions can change frequently and having to manually modify any and all dimensions associated with them can be overwhelming and inefficient. In addition, some dimensional changes might impact more than one part model. By ensuring that all features and parts are built with the required design intent, you can save time and create more robust models.

The size and shape of a part might evolve as you put an assembly together. Rather than switch frequently between several files to edit the parts, you can enable adaptivity. This enables you to specify geometric entities of part features to change, while controlling the size or location of other entities in an assembly. When you edit an adaptive part in the assembly, the adaptive components update accordingly.

Assembly Equations

Equations are user-defined mathematical relationships between parameters, that capture and control design intent in components. Equations can be between dimensions in a part or between assembly components. Assembly-level equations can drive dimensions and parameters in one component and equate them to dimensions and parameters in other components. This can be accomplished using derived components, linked spreadsheets, adaptivity, or a combination of these tools.

Component Generators

Component Generators enable you to create common components and perform calculations for them based on mechanical attributes. Component Generators rely on the Content Center for their geometric designs while using references inside the assembly.

Frame Generator

Frame Generator enables you to create the parts in a structural framework. The frame components use predefined cross-sections in the software and are generated based on geometry in a reference model.

Chapter Review Questions

1. What problems are associated with the bottom-up design approach? (Select all that apply.)

   a. Interference or misalignment between components.

   b. Incomplete design.

   c. Modifications to components must be manually propagated throughout the assembly.

2. Which is not an advantage of the top-down design approach?

   a. Organizes and helps enforce interactions and dependencies between components in an assembly.

   b. Creates part geometry independent of the assembly or any other component.

   c. Forces you to consider all areas of a final model before creating any geometry.

   d. Helps create clean, reusable geometry that interacts as expected with the rest of the assembly.

3. Which is not a top-down design technique that is available as functionality in the Autodesk Inventor software?

   a. Adaptive Modeling

   b. Layout Design

   c. Skeletal Modeling

   d. Multi-Body Design

4. You can create 3D models from sketch blocks that were created in the Layout Design?

   a. True

   b. False

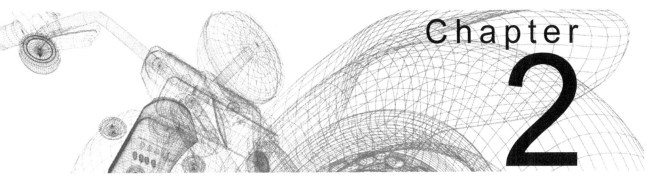

Chapter 2

Multi-Body Modeling

Multi-body modeling is a Top-down design technique where you create single part file in the context of an assembly model. Multi-body part files enable you to create your entire assembly design in the part environment using part modeling feature commands.

Learning Objectives in this Chapter

- Describe the advantages of building a part file using multiple solid bodies.
- Create solid bodies and correctly assign features to specific solid bodies.
- Modify the various solid bodies in a model by moving, removing, splitting, combining, or redefining them.
- Create new parts and assemblies from the multi-bodies in a single part.
- Individually control the visibility of and access to the properties for various solid bodies.

2.1 Multi-Body Part Modeling

Multi-body part files enable you to create your entire assembly design in the part environment using part modeling feature commands. This technique is commonly used when creating complex plastic or cast parts that require very intricate geometry. The design is arranged into separate bodies in the single part file. Figure 2–1 shows a model that has two solid bodies. **Solid2** is highlighted on the model. These separate bodies can then be extracted into individual parts for a new assembly.

Features can be shared between different bodies.

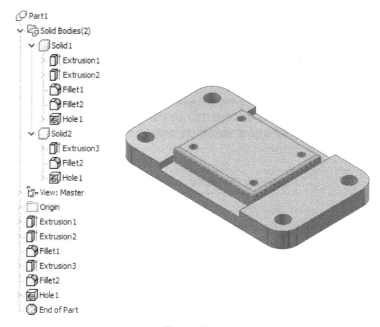

Figure 2–1

The advantages of building a part file using multi-bodies include the following:

- You do not need to create an initial complex file and directory structure to design parts in the context of a top-level assembly. The entire design resides in a single file and bodies are later extracted to create parts.

- A complex part file can be better organized using separate bodies with respect to their function or position in the model.

- Relationships between bodies can be set up and broken.

- You can control the visibility of bodies as a group rather than at the individual feature level.

- This method is useful for plastic part design, where interior components for a predefined shape can be designed in context and then extracted.

Creating the First Solid Body

With the creation of the first feature in any part file, the first solid body is automatically created. This is because  (New Solid) is automatically selected in the feature creation dialog box and mini-toolbar, as shown in Figure 2–2. Once the base feature is created, the *Solid Bodies* folder displays in the Model Browser and the first solid body is added to the folder.

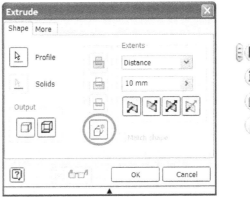

Figure 2–2

Creating Additional Solid Bodies

Once the first solid body is added to the model, each additional feature is automatically applied to it, unless a new feature is explicitly set to be created as a new solid body. To create a new solid body, create its feature as you normally would, but click

 (New Solid) in the feature creation dialog box or in the mini-toolbar. Once selected, a second body is added.

Assigning Features to Solid Bodies

Once two or more solid bodies are in a model, the selection of the placement/sketch planes are important to correctly locate the new feature in the required solid body. Consider the following:

- When creating a sketched feature, it is by default added to the same solid body as that of the sketch plane. For features

  to be added to a different solid body, click ⬚ (Solids) in the feature dialog box and then select the required solid body.

- When creating a pick-and-place feature, it is by default added to the same solid body as the placement references. In the case of a fillet, for example, it is added to the same solid body as the parent feature of the placement edge. If multiple edges are selected that belong to multiple solid bodies, the feature is added to each solid body.

- When creating a sketch-based or pick-and-place feature, it is only extended through its parent solid body, even if the **Through All** depth is selected. For features to interact with another solid body, click ⬚ (Solids) in the feature dialog box and then select additional solid bodies to be included.

Manipulating Solid Bodies

Once multiple solid bodies exist in the model, you can further manipulate them. You can redefine them as part of another solid body, move them, split them, and combine them.

Redefining/Removing Features in Solid Bodies

Once a feature is created and assigned to a solid body, you can re-assign it to another solid body or remove a solid body from interacting with the feature. To do so, redefine the original feature and click ⬚ (Solids) to activate it. You can select the new solid to apply it to or, if you want to remove a solid body from the initial selection set, press and hold <Ctrl> and select the solid body to remove.

Moving Bodies

You might need to move the various bodies in a multi-body part.

*The **Move** command is only available when working with solid bodies.*

How To: Move a Solid Body

1. In the *3D Model* tab>expanded Modify panel, click ⬚ (Move Bodies). The Move Bodies dialog box opens.
2. Select the solid bodies to move. If you need to select multiple bodies, you must click ⬚ (Bodies) again after selecting the first body to select additional bodies.

3. Select a move operation using the drop-down list in the Move Bodies dialog box, as shown in Figure 2–3.

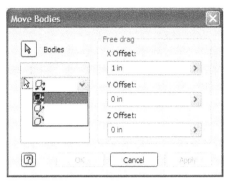

Figure 2–3

Each icon in the list enables you to move the body, as follows:

- **(Free drag):** Enables you to enter a precise X, Y, or Z offset value, or drag the preview in any direction.

- **(Move along ray):** Enables you to enter a precise offset value, or drag the preview offset from a selected reference.

- **(Rotate about line):** Enables you to enter a precise rotational angle value, or drag the preview around a selected axis.

4. Depending on the move operation selected, enter values and select references using the right side of the dialog box to define the movement.

5. To define a second move operation, if required, select **Click to add** and select a new move operation, as shown in Figure 2–4.

Figure 2–4

6. Continue to add move operations as required for the selected body.

*To edit the Move Body feature, right-click on it and select **Edit feature**.*

7. Click **OK** to complete the feature. A Move Body feature is added to the bottom of the Model Browser, as well as into each of the Solid Bodies selected to be moved.

Splitting Bodies

You can split a single body so that you can manipulate the resulting bodies independently.

How To: Split a Solid Body

*The **Split** command is available when working with solid bodies or Autodesk® Inventor® features.*

1. In the *3D Model* tab>Modify panel, click (Split).

2. Click (Split Solid) as the split method. The Split dialog box opens as shown in Figure 2–5.

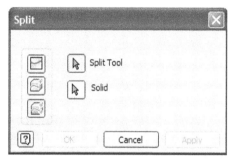

Figure 2–5

3. Select a work plane or a sketch as the *Split Tool*. The split tool defines where the split occurs.
4. Select the Solid body to split. If a sketch was selected as the split tool, the solid body to which the sketch plane belongs is automatically selected as the solid to be split. You can reselect this reference, as required.
5. Click **OK** to complete the split.

Combining Bodies

If you created two solid bodies separately during an initial design, you might decide later that they should be combined. Using the **Combine** command, you can add or remove material based on selected bodies.

How To: Combine Features

*The **Combine** command is only available when working with solid bodies.*

1. In the *3D Model* tab>Modify panel, click 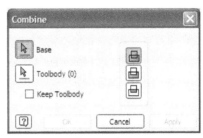 (Combine). The Combine dialog box opens as shown in Figure 2–6.

Figure 2–6

2. Select the solid body to use as the *Base* reference. The base body is the solid body on which the operation is going to be performed.
3. Select the solid body to use as the *Toolbody* reference. The toolbody is the solid body or bodies that is going to perform the operation.

You can only select one base body, but you can select multiple toolbodies, if required.

4. (Optional) To maintain the toolbody as a solid body after the operation, select **Keep Toolbody**. If you select this option, toolbody becomes invisible. This option is only available during the initial combine operation, not during the editing process.
5. Select an operation to perform on the base. The available operations include joining (⊟), cutting (⊟), and intersecting (⊟) the toolbody from the base.
6. Click **OK** to complete the feature. The Combine feature is listed at the bottom of the Model Browser and in the solid body used as the base reference.

Inserting Components into Parts

Using the **Derive** option, you can selectively include/exclude solid bodies (or other objects) from a source model to import it into a new or existing part file.

Refer to the Derived Components chapter for more information on this command.

Creating Parts from Part Bodies

You can extract individual bodies from a multi-body part into separate parts.

The steps for creating a part is similar to that for deriving a part.

How To: Extract a Body to Create a New Part

1. In the *Manage* tab>Layout panel, click 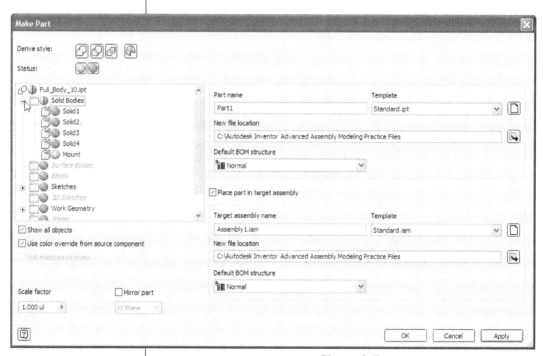 (Make Part). The Make Part dialog box opens as shown in Figure 2–7. Alternatively, you can select the bodies to be used in the Model Browser, right-click, and select **Make Part**.

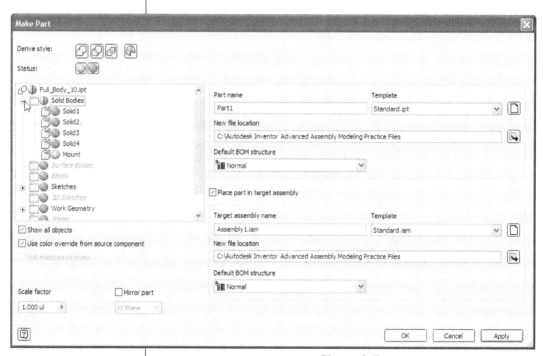

Figure 2–7

2. Select a Derive style icon from the top of the dialog box to define how to create the component. The icons are described as follows:

Icon	Description
	Create single solid body where seams between planar faces as removed.
	Create single solid body where seams between planar faces are kept.
	Keep each solid as an individual solid body.
	Create the body as a work surface.

3. Enable or disable which portions (e.g., solid bodies, sketches, parameters, etc.) of the model to use to create the new part by toggling the **Status** icons adjacent to the item name.

   *Use **Show all objects** to refine the tree in the Make Part dialog box to either show all objects that can be included/excluded, or to only list those headings that have applicable data in the solid body.*

   - A yellow circle with a plus symbol (⬤) indicates that the geometry is included in the new part.

   - A gray circle with a slash symbol (⬤) indicates that the geometry is not included in the new part.

   - A circle that is half yellow and half gray (⬤) indicates that some geometry within the object type is included, while some is not.

4. Define the remaining options on the right side of the Make Part dialog box to fully define the new part (e.g., part name, template to use, etc.).

5. (Optional) If you require the part to be in a new assembly, select **Place part in target assembly** and enter the assembly information.

6. Click **OK** to complete the part. Depending on the *Derive style* selected, the new part might combine the selected bodies into a single body, or keep each body separate.

The newly created part remains associative to the multi-body part, unless you explicitly break the link. In the newly created part, right-click on the source part name that has been imported and select **Break Link With Base Component**. The link can be suppressed (instead of broken) by selecting **Suppress Link With Base Component**.

Creating Components from Part Bodies

Selected bodies in a multi-body part can be extracted into separate components that are combined in a new top-level assembly.

How To: Extract Solid Bodies and Create a New Assembly from Them

1. In the *Manage* tab>Layout panel, click (Make Components). The Make Components: Selection dialog box opens. Alternatively, you can select the bodies to be used in the Model Browser, right-click, and select **Make Components**.
2. Select the solid bodies to extract in the Model Browser. All selected solid bodies are listed in the dialog box.
3. Ensure that the **Insert components in target assembly** option is selected.
4. Specify the remaining options on the right side of the Make Components: Selection dialog box to fully define the new component (e.g., target assembly name, template to use, etc.). The dialog box displays similar to that shown in Figure 2–8 once components have been selected.

*Consider using the **Make Component** command and disabling the **Insert components in target assembly** option instead of using the **Make Part** command multiple times when creating more than one component from a multi-body part.*

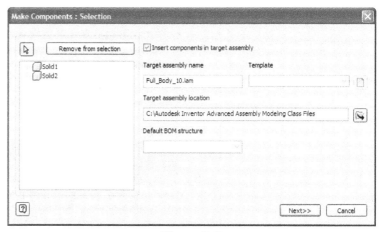

Figure 2–8

5. Click **Next**. The Make Components: Bodies dialog box opens.

The solid body name in the source model is used as the default name for the component.

6. Using the Make Components: Bodies dialog box, you can make changes to individual components that are being created as part of the assembly. You can click in each column to rename the resulting component, or change its template or BOM Structure. The dialog box opens similar to that shown in Figure 2–9.

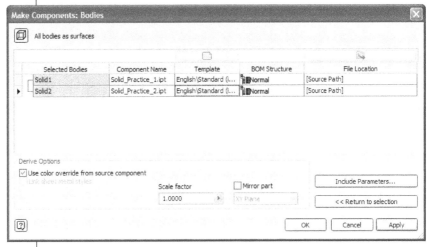

Figure 2–9

7. Set the options in the *Derive Options* area, as required.
8. Click **OK** to complete the operation.

The newly created parts and assembly remain associative to the multi-body part unless you explicitly break the link to the parent model. To break the link, you must open each created component, then right-click on the source part name that has been imported and select **Break Link With Base Component**. The link can be suppressed instead of broken by selecting **Suppress Link With Base Component**.

Solid Body Display

To control the visibility of a solid body, right-click on the solid body and enable or disable the **Visibility** option.

Solid Body Properties

To access the properties for a solid body, right-click on the solid body name and select **Properties**. The Body Properties dialog box opens as shown in Figure 2–10.

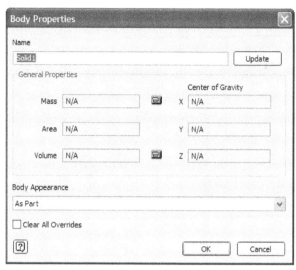

Figure 2–10

Using the Body Properties dialog box, you can do the following:

*The **Clear All Overrides** option removes color overrides from individual faces contained in the solid body.*

- Rename the solid body. You can also rename a solid body directly in the Model Browser.

- Update and provide the general properties for the solid body.

- Set a color style for the solid body.

Practice 2a

Multi-Body Part Design

Practice Objectives

- Create multiple solid bodies in a single part, and modify and add features to specific bodies.
- Create new part files by extracting solid bodies from a single part.

In this practice, you will create a single part file containing two solid bodies. In creating these solid bodies, you will learn to create multiple bodies in a model, add features to the bodies, and make changes to the bodies. To complete the practice, you will extract the solid bodies from the part file to create two individual part files. The completed model is shown in Figure 2–11.

Figure 2–11

Task 1 - Create a new model.

1. In the *Get Started* tab>Launch panel, click (Projects) to open the Projects dialog box. Project files identify folders that contain the required models.

This project file is used for the entire training guide.

2. Click **Browse**. In the *C:\Autodesk Inventor 2018 Design Tools and Strategies Practice Files* folder, select **Design Variations and Representations.ipj**. Click **Open**. The Projects dialog box updates and a check mark displays next to the new project name, indicating that it is the active project. The project file tells Autodesk Inventor where your files are stored. Click **Done**.

3. Start a new part model using the **Standard (in).ipt** template.

4. Create a new 2D Sketch on the XY Plane.

5. In the *Sketch* contextual tab>Create panel, click 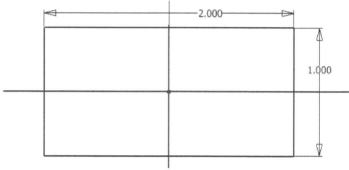 (Project Geometry) and select the YZ and XZ planes from the **Origin** node in the Model Browser.

6. In the *Sketch* contextual tab>Create panel, click

   (Rectangle) and sketch a rectangular entity approximately centered on the origin, as shown in Figure 2–12.

7. In the *Sketch* contextual tab>Constrain panel, click

   (Dimension) and create the 2 and 1 inch dimensions, as shown in Figure 2–12.

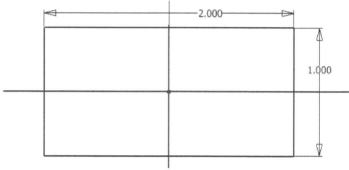

Figure 2–12

8. In the Constrain panel, click and set the two horizontal entities as symmetric about the XZ plane. Also set the two vertical entities as symmetric about the YZ plane.

Assigning a parameter name to a dimension directly in the Edit Dimension dialog box prevents having to do so in the Parameters dialog box.

9. With the sketch still active, double-click on the 2.000 dimension and type **width=2in**, as shown in Figure 2–13.

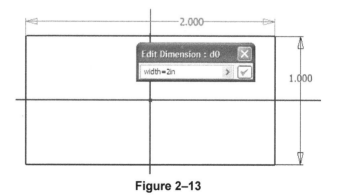

Figure 2–13

10. Double-click on the 1.000 dimension and type **depth=1in**.

11. Finish the sketch.

12. In the *3D Model* tab>Create panel, click  (Extrude).

13. Extrude the rectangular sketch a distance of 0.5 inches by typing **Height=0.5in** as the distance value. Note that

     (New Solid) is selected automatically in the mini-toolbar as shown in Figure 2–14, and in the dialog box because it is the first feature in the model and the first solid body must be created at the same time as the first feature.

You can also enter the distance value in the Extrude dialog box.

⊞ ⊢⊣▼	Height=0.5in ▶

🔍 Profile ▼

▢▼ ⌖▼ ▷▼

✓ ✕ ☰▼

Figure 2–14

14. Complete the extrude.

15. Review the Model Browser, as shown in Figure 2–15. **Extrusion1** displays below the **Origin**, as it is a feature of the part. Expand the **Solid Bodies** node and note that currently, there is only one Solid Body in the model, called **Solid1**. Expand **Solid1** and **Extrusion1** displays there as well.

⬡ Part1
  ⌄ 🔲 Solid Bodies(1)
    ⌄ ▢ Solid1
      > ⬡ Extrusion1
    > 🔲 View: Master
    > ▢ Origin
    > ⬡ Extrusion1
    └ ◉ End of Part

Figure 2–15

Task 2 - Create additional features in the model.

1. Create a new sketch on the surface shown in Figure 2–16.

2. In the *Sketch* contextual tab>Create panel, click (Project Geometry) and select the YZ plane from the Origin.

3. In the *Sketch* contextual tab>Create panel, click (Line) and sketch the linear entity shown in Figure 2–16. Align it to the YZ work plane through the center of the model.

4. Project the edge shown in Figure 2–16 to create a closed sketch. The entities at the top and bottom are automatically projected when the line is added.

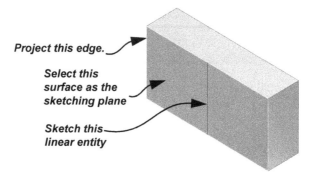

Project this edge.

Select this surface as the sketching plane

Sketch this linear entity

Figure 2–16

5. Finish the sketch.

6. In the *3D Model* tab>Create panel, click (Extrude).

7. Click (Cut) in the mini-toolbar or in the dialog box and select the left section to remove.

8. Type **Cutdepth=Height/2** as the distance value. Note that (New Solid) is not selected, because this is the second feature in the model and it defaults to being a feature in the first solid body.

9. Complete the extrude.

10. In the *3D Modify* panel>Modify panel, click (Fillet) and add two **.125 in** fillets to the geometry, as shown in Figure 2–17.

11. Review the Model Browser. **Extrusion2** and **Fillet1** have been added after **Extrusion1**. Expand the **Solid Bodies** node. Note that only one Solid Body, **Solid1**, is currently still in the model, and that **Extrusion2** and **Fillet1** have been added there as well. **Extrusion1**, **Extrusion2**, and **Fillet1** are all features in **Solid1**. The model and the Model Browser display as shown in Figure 2–17.

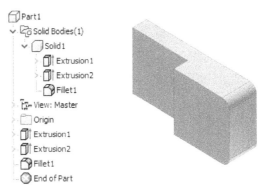

Figure 2–17

Task 3 - Review the modified parameter names.

1. In the Manage tab>Parameters panel, click

   f_x (Parameters). The Parameters dialog box opens as shown in Figure 2–18. The parameter names and equations that were entered during model creation are assigned in the dialog box.

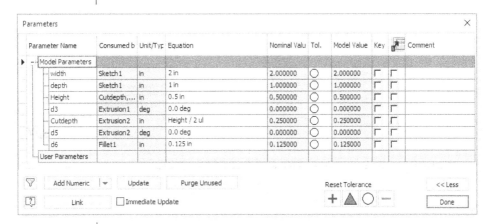

Figure 2–18

2. Close the Parameters dialog box.

Task 4 - Create a second solid body in the model.

1. Create a 2D sketch on the lower surface of the model that was just cut away.

2. Sketch a spline similar to that shown in Figure 2–19.

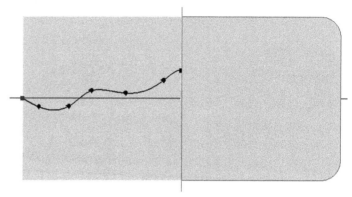

Figure 2–19

3. Project the required edges to create a closed sketch above the spline. Ensure that the spline and projected edges are constrained as **Coincident**.

4. Finish the sketch.

5. In the *3D Model* tab>Create panel, click (Extrude). Select the upper section of the sketch as the section to extrude.

6. Click (New Solid) in the mini-toolbar or in the Extrude dialog box to create the extrude feature as a separate solid body.

7. Type **Height** as the distance value. This creates a relationship between the two features.

8. Complete the feature.

9. Review the Model Browser. **Extrusion3** has been added after **Fillet1**. Expand the **Solid Bodies** node and note that two Solid Bodies are now in the model. **Extrusion1**, **Extrusion2**, and **Fillet1** are all features in **Solid1**, and **Extrusion3** is in **Solid2**. A re-oriented version of the model and the Model Browser display as shown in Figure 2–20.

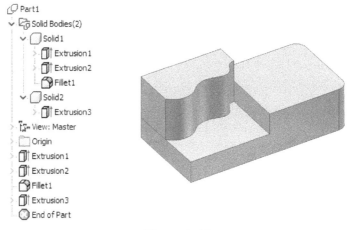

Figure 2–20

Task 5 - Modify the properties of a solid body.

---

1. In the Model Browser, right-click on **Solid2** (under the **Solid Bodies** node) and select **Properties**.

You can assign a new name to the solid body in the Body Properties dialog box.

2. In the Body Appearance drop-down list, select **Blue - Wall Paint - Glossy** to change the color of **Solid2**.

3. Click **Update** to update the mass, area, and volume of this single body.

4. Click **OK** to close the Body Properties dialog box.

Task 6 - Add features to the solid bodies.

1. In the *3D Model* tab>Modify panel, click 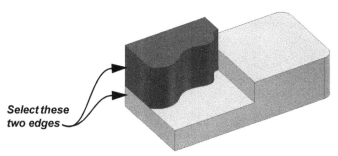 (Fillet) and select the two edges shown in Figure 2–21. The two edges are from different solid bodies. Ensure the value for the radius of the fillets is set to **0.125 in**.

Select these two edges

Figure 2–21

2. Complete the feature.

3. Review the Model Browser. **Fillet2** has been added after **Extrusion3**, as well as to both of the solid bodies. A re-oriented version of the model and the Model Browser display as shown in Figure 2–22. The benefit of having them created together is that if the value changes, both update. If you want them separated, you must create them as separate features.

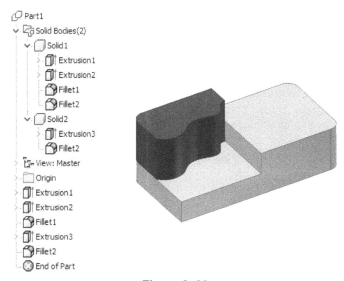

Figure 2–22

4. Re-orient the model to display the bottom of the model, as shown in Figure 2–23.

5. Create a sketch on the bottom surface and create three points at the centers of the fillets, as shown in Figure 2–23.

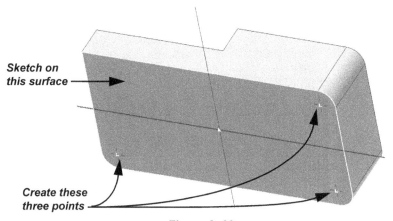

Sketch on this surface

Create these three points

Figure 2–23

6. Complete the sketch.

7. Use **From Sketch** to create holes at all three points. Set the *Termination* to **Through All** and type **.125in** for the *Diameter*.

8. Complete the feature.

9. Rotate the model, as shown in Figure 2–24, and note that the holes extrude through all of **Solid1** but not through **Solid2**. **Hole1** is listed as a feature in the Model Browser and a feature under the **Solid1 Solid Bodies** node. A feature is automatically added to the body from which the sketch plane is selected.

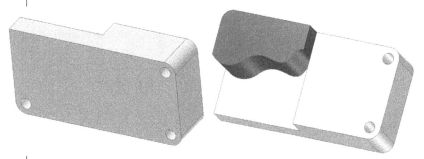

Figure 2–24

10. Double-click on **Hole1** in either location in the Model Browser to edit the hole.

11. In the Hole dialog box, click ⌇ (Solids) and select **Solid2** to include the holes as part of this solid body. All sketched features enable you to assign the feature to multiple bodies.

12. Complete the feature. The holes now extrude through both solid bodies, as shown in Figure 2–25.

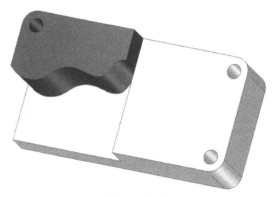

Figure 2–25

13. Save the model as **solid body practice.ipt**.

Task 7 - Extract the solid bodies to create two new part files.

1. In the *Manage* tab>Layout panel, click ▦ (Make Components).

    • When creating more than one component from a multi-body, the **Make Components** command, with the **Insert components in target assembly** option cleared, can be more efficient than using the **Make Part** command multiple times.

Alternatively, you can select both Solid1 and Solid2 in the Model Browser, right-click, and select Make Components.

2. In the Model Browser, in the **Solid Bodies** node, select **Solid1** and **Solid2**.

3. Clear the **Insert components in target assembly** option. The Make Components: Selection dialog box displays as shown in Figure 2–26.

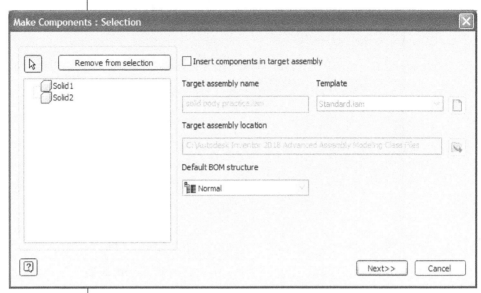

Figure 2–26

4. Click **Next**.

5. In the Make Components: Bodies dialog box, select **Solid1.ipt** and modify the *Component Name* to **Solid_Practice_1.ipt**.

6. Modify the name of *Solid2* to **Solid_Practice_2.ipt**.

7. In the *Solid1* row, select **Standard.ipt** and click

8. Select the **Standard (in).ipt** template and click **OK**.

9. Ensure that **Solid2** is also using the **Standard (in).ipt** template. The dialog box displays as shown in Figure 2–27.

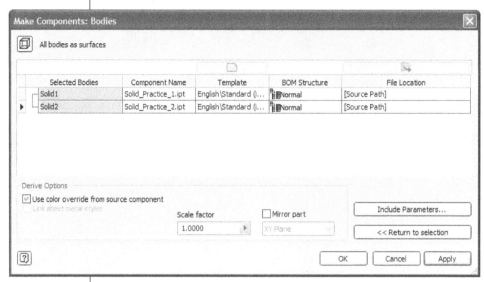

Figure 2–27

10. Click **OK**.

11. Save the changes to **Solid_Practice_1.ipt** and its dependents.

12. Open both **Solid_Practice_1.ipt** and **Solid_Practice_2.ipt** and review the results.

Task 8 - Modify reference part file.

1. Activate the **solid body practice.ipt** window.

2. Modify the **Height** parameter to **1** using the Parameters dialog box or by editing the dimensions associated with **Extrusion1**. Changes to both **Solid1** and **Solid2** are due to the relationships that you set while entering the original values for the features.

3. Activate the **Solid_Practice_1.ipt** window.

4. In the Quick Access Toolbar, click (Update) to update the model with the changes.

5. Activate and update **Solid_Practice_2.ipt**.

6. Save and close all part files.

Practice 2b

Derive Multi-Body Parts

Practice Objectives

- Create solid bodies in a part by deriving them from external parts.
- Modify the location of solid bodies in a single part, and combine multiple solid bodies into a single solid body.
- Create a new part file by extracting a solid body from another part.
- Create a new assembly file, along with its new part files, by extracting solid bodies from a single part.

In this practice, you will add solid bodies to a part by deriving the bodies from other parts. You will also learn to move and combine existing bodies in a multi-body part. To complete the practice, you will extract solid bodies from the multi-body part to create separate parts and an assembly. The completed model is shown in Figure 2–28.

Figure 2–28

Task 1 - Open part files.

1. Open **Full_Body_10.ipt**. The model displays as shown in Figure 2–29. Expand the **Solid Bodies** node and note that the file contains four solid bodies.

Figure 2–29

2. Open **Guide_Bracket_10.ipt**. The model displays as shown in Figure 2–30 and contains two solid bodies.

Figure 2–30

Task 2 - Change solid body names

1. With the **Guide_Bracket_10.ipt** model still active, right-click on **Solid1** under the **Solid Bodies** node of the Model Browser, and select **Properties**.

2. In the Body Properties dialog box, change the *Name* of **Solid1** to **Mounting Holes**, as shown in Figure 2–31. Click **OK**.

Figure 2–31

3. Right-click on **Solid2** under the **Solid Bodies** node of the Model Browser, and select **Properties**. Rename the solid body as **Groove Wall**.

4. Save and close **Guide_Bracket_10.ipt**.

Task 3 - Derive solid bodies from external part files.

1. In the *Manage* tab>Insert panel, click  (Derive).

2. In the Open dialog box, select **Guide_Bracket_10.ipt** and click **Open**. The Derived Part dialog box opens as shown in Figure 2–32.

Figure 2–32

3. Verify that  (Maintain each solid as a solid body) is selected and accept all other defaults. Click **OK**.

4. Rotate the model to the position shown in Figure 2–33.

Figure 2–33

5. Review the solid bodies in the Model Browser. The part now contains six multi-bodies, four from the original model and two from the derived part.

6. Expand the two new solid bodies in the Model Browser. The descriptions indicate the name of the original solid body, as well as the part file name from which it was derived. The derived part is also listed at the bottom of the Model Browser.

7. Change the names of these two new solid bodies to **Mount** and **Wall**.

Task 4 - Move bodies.

---

1. In the *3D Model* tab>expanded Modify panel, click  (Move Bodies). The Move Bodies dialog box opens.

2. Select both solid bodies, **Mount** and **Wall**. You must click  (Bodies) again after you select the first body in order to select the second body.

3. Set the *X Offset* to **-68mm**, the *Y Offset* to **2mm,** and the *Z Offset* to **0mm**.

4. Select **Click to add** and click 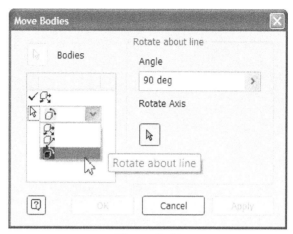 (Free drag) in the new row.

   Select (Rotate about line) in the drop-down list, as shown in Figure 2–34.

Figure 2–34

5. Select the edge shown in Figure 2–35 for the *Rotate Axis*. Change the *Angle* to **-90** and click **OK**.

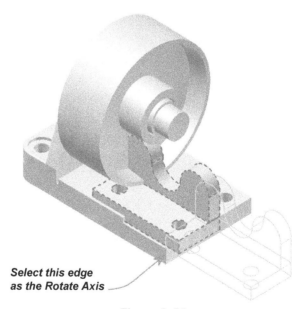

Select this edge as the Rotate Axis

Figure 2–35

*To edit the Move Body feature, right-click on it and select **Edit feature**.*

6. The **Move Body** feature is now listed at the bottom of the Model Browser and in both the **Mount** and **Wall** solid bodies. The model displays as shown in Figure 2–36.

Figure 2–36

Task 5 - Combine bodies.

1. In the *3D Model* tab>Modify panel, click (Combine). The Combine Body dialog box opens.

2. Select **Mount** as the *Base* reference, and **Wall** as the *Toolbody* reference.

3. Ensure that the **Keep Toolbody** option is not selected and click **OK**.

4. The **Combine** feature is now listed at the bottom of the Model Browser and in the **Mount** solid body. The **Wall** solid body has been consumed by **Mount**.

5. Save **Full_Body_10.ipt**.

Task 6 - Extract a new separate part from a solid body.

1. In the *Manage* tab>Layout panel, click (Make Part). The Make Part dialog box opens.

2. Click (Single solid body merging out seams between planar faces) as the *Derive style* at the top of the dialog box.

3. Expand the **Solid Bodies** node. Click next to **Solid1**, **Solid2**, and **Mount** to include the body in the new derived part. The icons adjacent to these bodies update to .

4. Type **Whole_Base** for the *Part name* and set the *Template* to **Standard (in).ipt**.

5. Clear the **Place part in target assembly** option.

6. Keep all other defaults. The Make Part dialog box opens as shown in Figure 2–37.

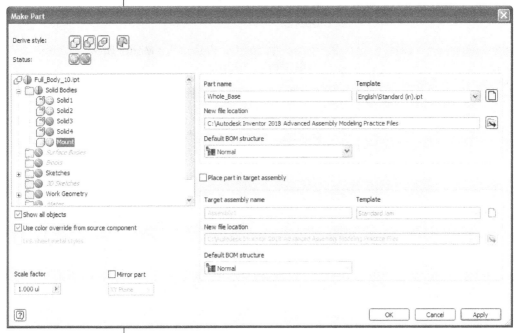

Figure 2–37

7. Click **OK** to complete the command. If you are prompted with a warning about saving a file, click **OK**. The resulting part file opens, containing a single solid body, as shown in Figure 2–38.

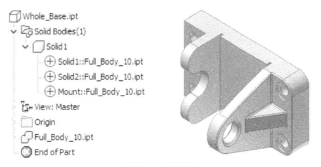

Figure 2–38

8. Save and close **Whole_Base.ipt**.

Task 7 - Make an assembly with parts.

1. Activate the **Full_Body_10.ipt** window if it is not already active.

2. In the *Manage* tab>Layout panel, click 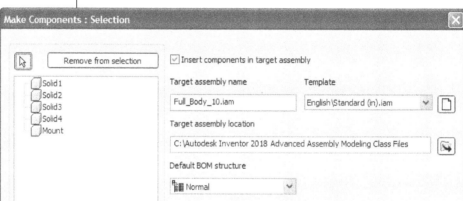 (Make Components). The Make Components: Selection dialog box opens.

Alternatively, you can select all the solid bodies in the Model Browser, right-click, and select **Make Components**.

3. Select all solid bodies in the Model Browser from **Full_Body_10.ipt**.

4. Set the template to **Standard (in).iam**.

5. Ensure that the **Insert components in target assembly** option is selected. The dialog box opens as shown in Figure 2–39.

Figure 2–39

6. Click **Next**. The Make Components: Bodies dialog box opens.

7. In the *Component Name* column, the name of the part is the same as the selected solid body name, as shown in Figure 2–40. These can be changed if required. For this practice, you can leave the default names.

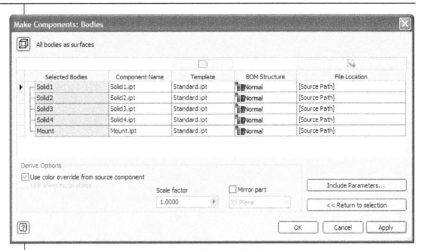

Figure 2–40

8. Click **OK** without making any changes in the Make Components: Bodies dialog box. A new assembly called **Full_Body_10.iam** with five parts is created. The part names are based on the solid body names, as shown in Figure 2–41. Each of these parts are initially grounded. You can unground components and constrain them as required.

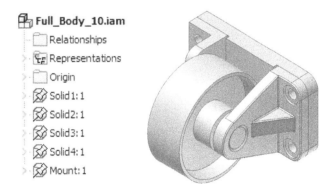

Figure 2–41

9. Save and close all files.

Chapter Review Questions

1. Multi-body part design requires the use of an assembly. Parts are created within the context of the assembly.

   a. True

   b. False

2. How are the second and any subsequent solid bodies created in a model?

   a. Explicitly set a new feature to be created as a new solid body.

   b. Each new feature is automatically added as a new solid body.

   c. Use specific solid body commands in the ribbon prior to creating the feature.

   d. None of the above.

3. Which of the following buttons/options is used in the Extrude dialog box to ensure that an extruded cut extrudes through multiple solid bodies?

   a.

   b.

   c.

   d. **Through All** (extent option)

4. A single Fillet feature has been added to a model that currently has three solid bodies. An edge from each of the three solid bodies was selected as placement references. Which of the following statements is true regarding the model?

   a. A fourth solid body will be added to the model.

   b. The Fillet feature will be added to the solid body in which the first reference edge belongs.

   c. The Fillet feature will be added to each of the three solid bodies.

   d. The Fillet feature will cause the three solid bodies to combine into one.

5. Match the Move Body operation type in the left column with its symbol in the right column.

Answer

a. Rotate about line

_____

b. Free drag

_____

c. Move along ray

_____

6. Which of the following can be used as the split tool when splitting a solid body? (Select all that apply.)

a. Work Plane

b. Face

c. Sketch

d. Edge

7. Which solid body manipulation option enables you to create a single solid body from two solid bodies?

a. Union

b. Combine

c. Extrude

d. Split

8. Which of the following derive styles enables you to create a single solid body when using the **Make Part** command?

1   2   3

a. 1, 2, and 3

b. 1 and 2

c. 2 and 3

d. 1 and 3

Answers: 1.b, 2.a, 3.c, 4.c, 5.(bca), 6.(a,c), 7.b, 8.b

Command Summary

Button	Command	Location
	Combine	• **Ribbon**: *3D Model* tab>Modify panel
	Derive	• **Ribbon**: *Manage* tab>Insert panel
	Make Component	• **Ribbon**: *Manage* tab>Layout panel
	Make Part	• **Ribbon**: *Manage* tab>Layout panel
	Move Bodies	• **Ribbon**: *3D Model* tab>Modify panel
	Split	• **Ribbon**: *3D Model* tab>Modify panel

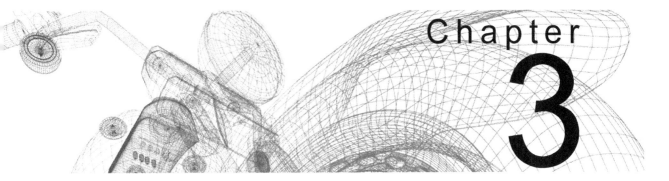

Derived Components

Derived components use an existing model as their base component. Features are copied from the base component into the new one to communicate design information. This information is then used to create the geometry in the new derived component.

Learning Objectives in this Chapter

- Derive new geometry in a part by importing and referencing objects from a source part.
- Describe the steps required to modify a derived component when updating it from its referenced model, adjusting the derived options, or breaking the associative link.

3.1 Derived Components

The **Derive Component** command enables you to create new geometry in a part by importing and referencing objects from a source model (i.e., a part or assembly). Based on the source geometry type, the newly created derived component is called either a derived part or derived assembly. When the source model changes, the derived part or assembly also changes.

General Steps

Use the following general steps to create a derived component:

1. Select a component to derive.
2. Select the derive style.
3. Select options for parts and assemblies.
4. Complete the operation.

Step 1 - Select a component to derive.

To create a derived part, create a new or open an existing part file. In the *Manage* tab>Insert panel, click (Derive) and open the part or assembly file from which to derive. The Derived Part or Derived Assembly dialog box opens, as shown in Figure 3–1.

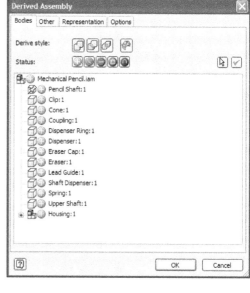

Figure 3–1

Step 2 - Select the derive style.

Select a *Derive style* icon from the top of the dialog box to define how to derive the component. The icons are as follows.

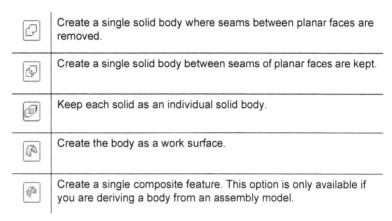

	Create a single solid body where seams between planar faces are removed.
	Create a single solid body between seams of planar faces are kept.
	Keep each solid as an individual solid body.
	Create the body as a work surface.
	Create a single composite feature. This option is only available if you are deriving a body from an assembly model.

Step 3 - Select options for parts and assemblies.

The available items that can be imported from the referenced part or assembly are listed in the tree structure in the dialog box (e.g., Sketches, 3D Sketches, Parameters, and iMates). For assemblies, it is listed on the *Other* tab. The items that you can import include the following:

The Composite Features option is only available when the source file already contains a derived assembly or composite feature.

- Solid Bodies
- Surface Bodies
- Blocks
- Sketches
- 3D Sketches

- Work Geometry
- iMates
- Parameters
- Composite Features

*To reduce the amount of clicks used to select all parts of a Derive, you can right-click on the assembly and select **Select All Parts**.*

Use this option to reduce memory consumption while maintaining a place holder for the component in the derived assembly.

To change the status of an item in the part or assembly dialog box (i.e., to include or exclude it), click on the symbol next to that item until it toggles to the required status symbol or select the item and click the Status icon. The options vary depending whether you are using the Derived Part or Assembly dialog box.

The Status symbols are described as follows:

- A yellow circle with a plus symbol ( ) indicates that the geometry is included in the derived part or assembly.

- A gray circle with a slash symbol ( ) indicates that the geometry is not included in the derived part or assembly.

- A red circle with a minus symbol ( ) indicates that the volume of that part is to be subtracted.

- A green circle with a square symbol ( ) indicates that the component is represented by a bounding box of the models size.

- A blue circle with an upside down U shape ( ) indicates that the selected component intersects with the derived part.

- A circle that is half yellow and half gray ( ) indicates that some geometry within the object type are included, while some are not.

Consider using the following options to further customize a derived part:

- Use **Show all objects** to refine the tree to show all objects that can be included/excluded. Clear the option to only see items previously set up in the originating component using the **Export Objects** command.

- By default, color overrides from the original part copy to the derived part. Clear the **Use color override from source component** option to remove this default behavior.

- Use **Link sheet metal styles** to include the sheet metal thickness and other parameters in the derived part

- Use **Reduced Memory Mode** to create a part using less memory. This option excludes source bodies from the cache to that no source bodies display in the Model Browser. If you break or suppress the link, the memory savings are lost.

- Use the Design View drop-down list to select the required representation to use.

- Adjust the size of the derived component using a scale factor.

- Use **Mirror Part** to mirror the component about a selected origin work plane (XY, YZ, or XZ).

The remaining tabs in the Derived Assembly dialog box are shown in Figure 3–2.

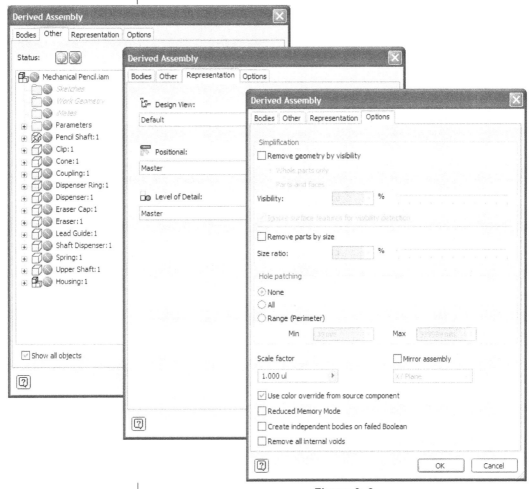

Figure 3–2

- Use the *Other* tab to include the items of the components in the derived assembly in the same manner as that for derived parts.

- Use the *Representation* tab to select the required representation to use.

- Use the *Options* tab to simplify model geometry, control hole patching, and scale or mirror an assembly. The following options are only found in the Derived Assembly dialog box:

Simplification	Use the options in this area to define what geometry is kept, based on its visibility status in the original component.
	By default, the Parts and faces of the original assembly are kept with a Visibility of 0%. Using this option, all faces that are not exposed in any view orientation are removed. Increase the Visibility percentage to remove parts or faces that have a specified percentage visible in any view orientation removed from the shrinkwrap part.
Remove parts by size	Use this option to remove geometry based on size. Any component smaller then the specified percentage of the overall assembly is removed.
Hole patching	Use this option to keep or remove holes. You can also remove holes of a specified size.
Create independent bodies on failed Boolean	Use this option to create a multi-body part when a single solid body cannot be generated.
Remove all internal voids	Use this option to fill all of the internal void shells in the derived solid body part.

Step 4 - Complete the operation.

Click **OK** to create the derived part and close the dialog box.

A derived component uses an existing part or assembly as its base feature and features can be added to it.

The original part is listed in the Model Browser as the base component. For a derived assembly, the components of the assembly that were included are combined into one part, but the individual components are listed, as shown in Figure 3–3. Individual components can still be suppressed.

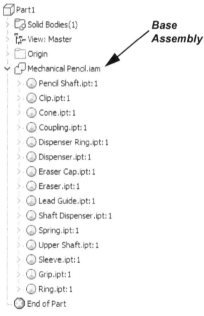

Figure 3–3

If you have the derived component open and you want to open the part or assembly that the derived component is referencing, right-click on it and select **Open Base Component**, or double-click on the base part or assembly in the Model Browser.

Once created, additional features can be added to a derived part or assembly (such as additional cuts and holes).

3.2 Modify Derived Components

Once a derived component is created, you can modify it in any of the following ways:

Update Derived Components

If changes are made to the referenced model, the symbol next to the base feature in the derived component changes to ⚡. This indicates that a change was made and an update is required. In the Quick Access Toolbar, click (Update) to update the derived component to match the referenced model.

Edit Derived Components

You can edit derived components once you finish creating them, if required. Editing derived components enables you to modify all of your selections made during the creation process.

How To: Edit a Derived Component

1. Right-click on the base part or assembly in the Model Browser and select **Edit Derived Part** or **Edit Derived Assembly**. The original dialog box opens.
2. Redefine the options, as required.
3. Click **OK**.

Break the Associative Link

You can break or suppress the associative link between the referenced model and the derived component so that changes to the referenced model no longer or temporarily affect the derived component. Right-click on the base part or assembly in the Model Browser and select either **Break Link with Base Component** or **Suppress Link with Base Component**. The icon for the base part or assembly displays in the Model Browser with a broken link icon or a suppressed link icon, as shown in Figure 3–4.

A suppressed link can be unsuppressed at any time, but a broken link cannot be re-established.

Figure 3–4

Practice 3a

Derived Components

Practice Objectives

- Create a new component derived from an assembly and then modify the base assembly file and update the derived component.
- Redefine the options for a derived component.
- Break the link between a base assembly and its derived component.

In this practice, you will create a derived part from an assembly. The derived part is edited, and changes are made to investigate how it affects the other components. The assembly and derived parts are shown in Figure 3–5.

Figure 3–5

Task 1 - Create a new component derived from an assembly.

1. Open **Derive Assem.iam**. The model displays in Isometric view. The assembly consists of four parts. This assembly will act as the reference for the derived part.

2. Create a new part using the **Standard(mm).ipt** template.

3. In the *Manage* tab>Insert panel, click (Derive).

4. In the Open dialog box, select the **Derive Assem.iam** file to derive. Click **Open**.

5. Ensure that the Derive style is set to  (Single solid body merging out seams between planar faces). Keep the remaining default selections in the Derived Assembly dialog box to verify that all four components are included. Click **OK**. The model displays as shown in Figure 3–6.

Part1
> Solid Bodies(1)
> View: Master
> Origin
> Derive Assem.iam
End of Part

Figure 3–6

6. Save the derived part as **Derived Part.ipt**. The derived part generated looks identical to the assembly, except it is only one file (a single part), compared to four individual part files placed in an assembly file. Right-click on the name of the file in the Model Browser and select **iProperties**. In the *General* tab, note the size of the file.

Task 2 - Modify the derived component settings.

1. Double-click on **Derive Assem.iam** in the derived part's Model Browser to open the base assembly file, or select its tab at the bottom of the main window if it is still open.

2. In the Model Browser, double-click on the part **102650** to open it in the context of the main assembly. In the Quick Access Toolbar, use the Color Override drop-down list to change its color from *Orange* to **Red**, as shown in Figure 3–7.

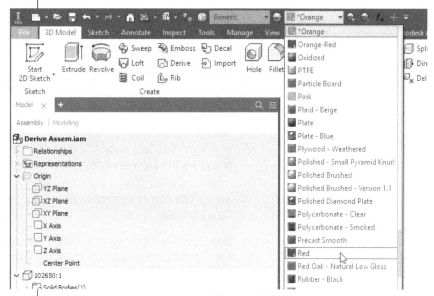

Figure 3–7

3. In the *3D Model* tab>Return panel, click 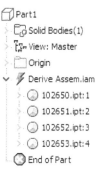 (Return) to return to the main assembly.

4. Save the assembly and click **OK** in the Save dialog box.

5. Switch to the **Derived Part.ipt** file by selecting its tab at the bottom of the main window.

6. The red lightning bolt icon (⚡) in front of **Derive Assem.iam** in the Model Browser, as shown in Figure 3–8, indicates a change was made to the original deriving component.

Part1
　Solid Bodies(1)
　View: Master
　Origin
　Derive Assem.iam
　　102650.ipt:1
　　102651.ipt:2
　　102652.ipt:3
　　102653.ipt:4
　End of Part

Figure 3–8

7. In the Quick Access Toolbar, click (Update) to update the derived part. The red lightning bolt is removed and **102650.ipt** displays in red.

8. Right-click on **Derive Assem.iam** in the Model Browser and select **Edit Derived Assembly**. The original Derived Assembly dialog box opens.

9. In the *Bodies* tab, click (Maintain each solid as a solid body) as the Derive style.

10. Select the *Representation* tab, clear (Associative) for the Design View.

11. Switch to the *Options* tab, select **Remove parts by size** in the *Simplification* area, and set the *Size ratio* to **40%**. Set the *Hole patching* option to **All**. Click **OK**. The model displays as shown in Figure 3–9.

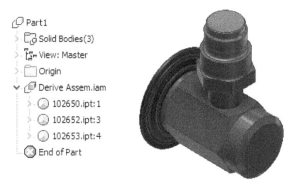

Figure 3–9

12. Note that the Solid Bodies node is now populated with

additional bodies because (Maintain each solid as a solid body) was selected. One component has also been removed from the assembly because of the size ratio setting, and the holes (or cavities) are now patched in the derived part. In

addition, by removing associativity ( ) to the Design Views, changes to color and visibilities will not update if they are modified in the original files.

13. Save the file and check its size in the iProperties. Note that the size of the file is now smaller.

14. Right-click on **Derive Assemb.iam** in the Model Browser and select **Edit Derived Assembly**. In the *Bodies* tab, select any one of the components currently included and click

 ⊚ (Includes bounding boxes of the selected components) to toggle the icons. Change the other two components to display as bounding boxes as well. Click **OK**. The model displays as shown in Figure 3–10.

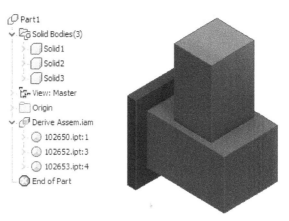

Figure 3–10

15. Note that the parts are replaced with bounding boxes that represent their size extents in a simplified manner. Save the file again and check its size in the iProperties. Note that the size of the file is considerably smaller.

16. Right-click on **Derived Assem.iam** in the Model Browser and select **Suppress Link With Base Component**.

 ⧉ (Suppressed Link) displays in front of the assembly in the Model Browser.

17. Attempt to open the base assembly by double-clicking on **Derived Assem.iam** in the Model Browser. Note that it will not initiate because the link has been suppressed. The **Edit Derived Assembly** is also no longer available in the shortcut menu, as shown in Figure 3–11.

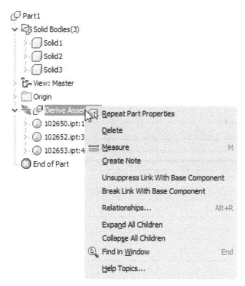

Figure 3–11

18. In the Model Browse, right-click on **Derived Assem.iam** and select **Break Link With Base Component**. 🔖 (Broken Link) displays in front of the assembly in the Model Browser.

19. In the Model Browse, right-click on **Derived Assem.iam** and note that an option is not available to redefine the link to the original file. Only executing the **Undo** command at this point will resolve the link to the original file. Performing a save and exiting will permanently disassociate the geometry. Breaking a link is beneficial if the original files do not need to be referenced again, but it is important to ensure this before breaking the link.

20. Save and close the files.

Chapter Review Questions

1. Additional feature geometry can be added to a model that has been created based on derived geometry from another model.

   a. True

   b. False

2. Which of the following items cannot be imported from the referenced part or assembly?

   a. Parameters

   b. Solid Bodies

   c. Composite Features

   d. Drawings

3. Match the symbols used to create a derived part (in the right column) with their definition shown in the left column.

		Answer
a. The geometry is included in the derived part.	⬤	_____
b. Some geometry is included while some is not included in the derived part.	⬤	_____
c. The geometry is not included in the derived part.	⬤	_____

4. Match the symbols used to create a derived assembly (in the right column) with their definition shown in the left column.

Answer

a. The component is represented by a bounding box. _____

b. The volume is to be subtracted from the derived assembly. _____

c. The selected component intersects with the derived assembly. _____

d. The geometry is not included in the derived assembly. _____

e. The geometry is included in the derived assembly. _____

f. Some geometry is included while some is not included in the derived assembly. _____

5. When deriving a part model into a new part file, which of the following can you use to customize the derived geometry? (Select all that apply.)

a. Select a specific Design View to derive from.

b. Select parameters to include in the new file.

c. Patch holes in the derived geometry.

d. Specify a scale factor to set a size for the derived geometry.

6. A link that is broken with the base component can be unbroken; however, a suppressed link cannot be unsuppressed.

a. True

b. False

Answers: 1.a, 2.d, 3.(acb), 4.(febadc), 5.(a,b,d), 6.b

Command Summary

Button	Command	Location
	Derive	• **Ribbon:** *Manage* tab>Insert panel
	Update	• **Quick Access Toolbar**

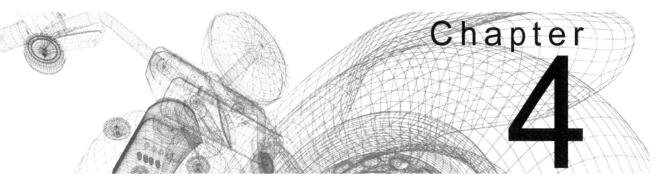

4

Layout Design

Layout Design is a top-down design tool. It can be used to convey a model's design intent (i.e., layout) using a 2D sketch. From the sketch, you can generate 3D models. Any changes made to the sketch update in the 3D models.

Learning Objectives in this Chapter

- Quickly convey the design intent of a model by creating and modifying layouts and sketch blocks.
- Define and test the kinematic motion of an assembly with the use of nested sketch blocks.
- Create 3D models from sketch blocks.

4.1 Layout Design

A layout is a top-down design tool that can be used to quickly convey the design intent of a model. A layout is a 2D sketch, as shown on the left in Figure 4–1, that provides a central repository for overall dimensions, spatial locations, and the general shape of components in a design. By generating 3D models based on the layout, as shown on the right in Figure 4–1, changes made to the layout are updated in the 3D models. This ensures that changes in design are accurately propagated to the entire assembly. Layouts can also be useful when working with a mechanized assembly. Through a layout, you can quickly define and test the kinematics of an assembly.

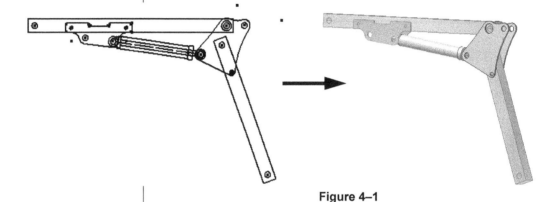

Figure 4–1

General Steps

Use the following general steps to create a layout.

1. Create a layout.
2. Define sketch blocks.
3. Make parts and components.

Step 1 - Create a layout.

You can create a layout in a part or an assembly file. To create a layout as a part file, create an empty part and define a 2D sketch as the layout. The layout is saved in the standard part file.

To create a layout in an assembly, click (Make Layout) (*Assemble* tab>expanded Component panel). The layout is automatically added to the active assembly as a grounded component, as shown in Figure 4–2. A new standard part file is generated.

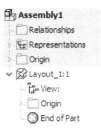

Figure 4–2

- All layout geometry must be created in the 2D Sketch environment. Create the sketch on one of the three Origin planes and add the entities required to represent the block.

Step 2 - Define sketch blocks.

An AutoCAD block can be translated into an Autodesk ®Inventor® sketch block.

A sketch block is a grouping of 2D geometry in the layout that represents a particular portion of the assembly (typically a component or a subassembly). You define each component in an assembly as a separate sketch block. You can then create sketch blocks that contain other sketch blocks (nested sketch blocks) to define subassemblies.

You must be in the Sketch environment to create a sketch block and the Layout panel must be displayed.

To create a sketch block, select the 2D entities that make up the sketch block. In the *Sketch* contextual tab>Layout panel, click

(Create Block). The Create Block dialog box is shown in Figure 4–3.

You can also select the geometry that makes up the sketch block after

clicking (Create Block).

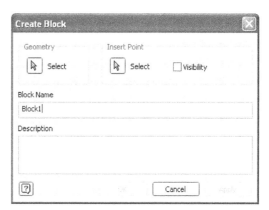

Figure 4–3

By default, the insert point is the center of the sketch block.

Enter a meaningful name for the sketch block and, if required, define an insert point and add a description. Click **OK** to create the block. Once created, the block is added to both the **Sketch** and the **Blocks** nodes of the Model Browser, as shown in Figure 4–4.

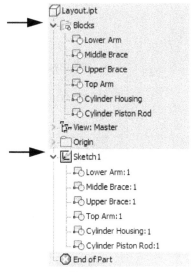

Figure 4–4

- Once defined, you can add constraints between sketch blocks to locate the them relative to each other. These constraints are converted into assembly constraints when 3D components are generated.

Changes made to the geometry in one sketch block updates in all instances of the sketch block.

- To add multiple instances of a sketch block to your layout, drag the existing sketch block from the Model Browser into the graphic window.

Nested Sketch Blocks

Nested Sketch Blocks are useful when defining and testing the kinematic motion of an assembly.

You can also create nested sketch blocks that become subassemblies when the 3D models are generated. To create a nested sketch block, create the sketch blocks first, then multi-select all the sketch blocks you want to nest and click

(Create Block).

The nested sketch block displays in the Model tree, as shown in Figure 4–5.

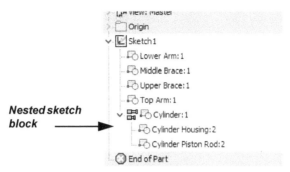

Nested sketch block ⟶

Figure 4–5

- By default, nested sketch blocks move together. Once the nested sketch block is created, right-click on it and ensure that the **Flexible** option is activated so that the blocks are able to move relative to each other to simulate kinematic motion.

Editing Sketch Blocks

Use the following methods to edit an existing sketch block:

- To add new geometry to an existing sketch block, double-click on the sketch block in the Model Browser to activate it. All geometry created is then automatically added to the active sketch block.

- To add existing geometry to an existing sketch block, double-click on the sketch block to activate it, select the geometry to add, then right-click and select **Add to Block**.

- To modify the name, insert point, or description of an existing sketch block, double-click on the sketch block to activate it. Click anywhere in the graphic window to ensure that no geometry is selected, right-click, and select **Block Properties**.

- To define the properties of a sketch block, right-click on the sketch block and select **Properties**. The Geometry Properties dialog box displays, as shown in Figure 4–6. You can define the color, line weight, and line type.

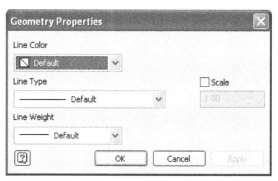

Figure 4–6

Step 3 - Make parts and components.

Using the **Make Part** and **Make Components** commands, you can quickly create 3D models from sketch blocks. The components remain associative to the layout. When changes are made to 2D sketch blocks, the 3D models also update.

Make Part

Use the **Make Part** command to create a single part file from one or more selected sketch blocks.

How To: Create a Part from a Sketch Block

You can also access the ***Make Part*** *command in the Manage tab>Layout panel.*

1. In the *Sketch* contextual tab>Layout panel, click (Make Part). Alternatively, you can select the blocks to be used in the Model Browser, right-click, and select **Make Part**. The Make Part dialog box opens.
2. Set the *Derive style* option. The options are the same as those used for the **Derive** command.
3. Select the sketch block from the **Sketches>Sketch** node in the tree, as shown in Figure 4–7. Alternatively, you can select the sketch blocks before activating the command.

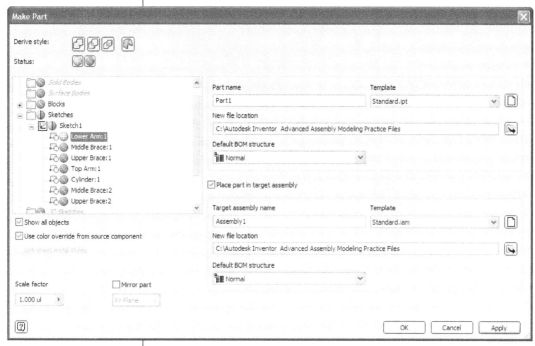

Figure 4–7

- The Make Part dialog box behaves similarly to the Derived Part dialog box; however, instead of adding the derived part into the active file, you create the derived part from the active file.

- Use the Make Part dialog box to define the part and, if required, the target assembly information. You can insert the part into an existing assembly or create a new target assembly.

4. Click **OK** to generate the model. The position of the generated component is based on the position of the source part relative to the part origin.

Make Components

The **Make Components** command creates multiple parts and assemblies in one operation.

How To: Create Multiple Components from Sketch Blocks

You can also access the ***Make Components*** *command in the Manage tab>Layout panel.*

1. In the *Sketch* contextual tab>Layout panel, click (Make Components). Alternatively, you can select the blocks to be used in the Model Browser, right-click, and select **Make Components**. The Make Components: Selection dialog box opens.

2. Select the sketch block(s) from the Model Browser. The blocks are added to the Make Components dialog box, as shown in Figure 4–8. Alternatively, you can select the sketch blocks before activating the command.

Figure 4–8

3. Specify the *Target assembly name* and *location* and click **Next**. The Make Components: Blocks dialog box opens, as shown in Figure 4–9. The dialog box lists each selected sketch block and provides information about the component it is going to generate.

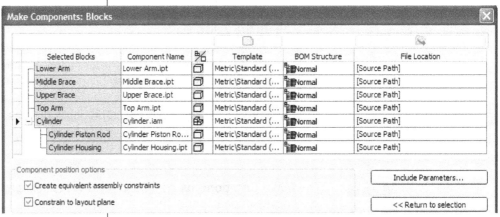

Figure 4–9

- You can change the information in the *Component Name*, *Template*, *BOM Structure*, or *File Location* columns of any of the components by clicking inside the appropriate cell.

- By default, all constraints created between sketch blocks are translated into assembly constraints. If you do not want to generate the assembly constraints, clear the **Create equivalent assembly constraints** option.

4. Click **OK** to generate the target assembly and the components.

- The first component in the new assembly is the Layout part. This part is grounded, as shown in Figure 4–10. Each sketch block is added to the assembly as a component.

- Any sketch constraints added between blocks are translated into assembly constraints between the 3D components and are shown in the Model Browser. The constraints might be active or suppressed, depending on the sketch constraints that were created in the Layout. A fourth Z Angle constraint is created and suppressed. When the **Constrain to layout plane** option is cleared, the XY Flush constraint is suppressed and the Z Angle constraint is activated.

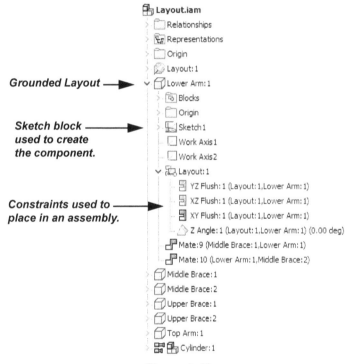

Figure 4–10

- Components remain associative to the layout. If a dimensional constraint in the Layout changes, it updates in the assembly. However, if you change a geometric constraint (i.e., add, remove, or modify), it does not update in the assembly. To update these changes, you must reapply the **Make Components** command on the affected components.

Changing Component Position

By default, all components are created along the Z-axis (the layout plane). You can offset the components from the layout plane once the components have been generated. To change the position of a component, consider the following:

- Use ⟨icon⟩ (Free Move) and ⟨icon⟩ (Free Rotate) in the *Assemble* tab>Position panel to freely move and rotate components along the X, Y, or Z axis. Alternatively, you can right-click on the component in the Model Browser to access the options. Select the command followed by the component and relocate it as required. These commands do not permanently reposition the components. Click ⟨icon⟩ (Local Update) to update the assembly to return the component to their original location.

- To change the position of a component relative to the XY plane, you must change the offset value associated with the XYFlush constraint for the component. Select it and enter a value at the bottom of the Model Browser. To change component positions in the XZ and YZ planes you must unsuppress their Flush constraints, select them, and enter offset values at the bottom of the Model Browser.

- All constraints that are created by default between components are created based on the constraints in the layout sketch. These constraints can be deleted and new constraints established, as required, to reposition components in the assembly.

Practice 4a

Layout Design

Practice Objectives

- Create multiple sketch blocks and nested sketch blocks.
- Constrain multiple sketch blocks to one another.
- Generate components and an assembly from existing sketch blocks in a layout, and convert them to 3D solid geometry.

In this practice, you will create a layout that is used to generate the assembly shown in Figure 4–11. You will use the layout to control both dimensional and positional changes.

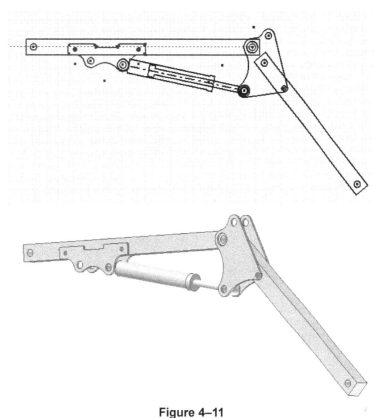

Figure 4–11

Task 1 - Open a layout.

1. Open **Layout.ipt**. The model displays as shown in
   Figure 4–12. The sketched geometry has already been
   created. Note that it has all been created in a single sketch. In
   the next task, you will edit the sketch and generate sketch
   blocks.

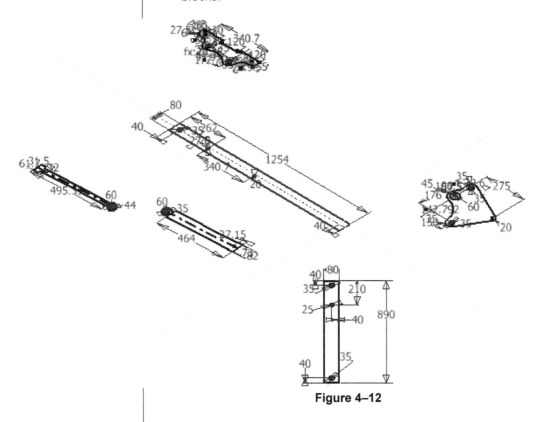

Figure 4–12

Task 2 - Create sketch blocks.

1. Double-click on **Sketch1** to edit it.

2. Reorient the sketch to **Front**, if it is not already done.

3. Right-click anywhere on the ribbon and select **Show Panels>
   Layout** to add the Layout panel to the ribbon, if not already
   displayed.

4. Select the geometry shown in Figure 4–13.

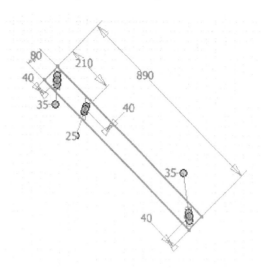

Figure 4–13

The Sketch tab is the active tab.

5. In the Layout panel, click  (Create Block).

6. Type **Lower Arm** in the *Block Name* field and click **OK**. The **Lower Arm** sketch block is added to both the **Blocks** and **Sketch1** nodes of the Model Browser, as shown in Figure 4–14.

Figure 4–14

7. Note the dimensions associated with the newly created block have disappeared from the screen. Select and drag the **Lower Arm** sketch block. All geometry that makes up the sketch block moves as a single entity.

8. Highlight all geometry labeled *Middle Bracket* in Figure 4–15 and click (Create Block).

9. In the *Block Name* field, type **Middle Bracket** and then click **Apply**.

10. Continue creating sketch blocks for the geometry, as shown in Figure 4–15.

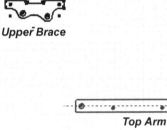

Upper Brace

Middle Bracket

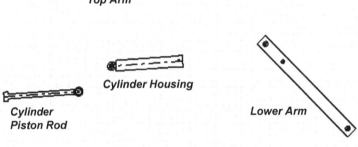

Top Arm

Cylinder Housing

Cylinder Piston Rod

Lower Arm

Figure 4–15

11. Once all of the blocks have been created, click **Cancel** to close the Create Block dialog box.

12. The **Middle Bracket** sketch block has been named incorrectly. Double-click on the **Middle Bracket** sketch block to activate it.

13. Click anywhere in the graphic window to clear any geometry that might be selected. Right-click in the graphic window and select **Block Properties**.

14. Change the name of the block to **Middle Brace** and click **OK** to confirm the change and close the dialog box. Alternatively, you can also rename the block in the Model Browser.

15. In the Exit panel, click ![Finish Edit Block icon] (Finish Edit Block).

16. The *Sketch* tab should still be the active tab. If not, double-click on the sketch to activate it. If you had selected the block from the **Blocks** node, the sketch would have been deactivated.

Task 3 - Create a sketch constraint.

1. Click ![Collinear Constraint icon] (Collinear Constraint) to add a collinear constraint between the two centerlines of the **Cylinder Piston Rod** and **Cylinder Housing** sketch blocks, as shown in Figure 4–16.

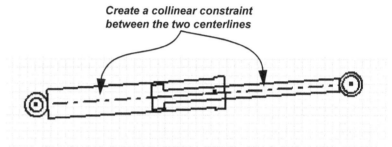

Create a collinear constraint between the two centerlines

Figure 4–16

2. Select the **Cylinder Piston Rod** in the graphic window and drag. A simple kinematic motion has been created using the collinear constraint.

Task 4 - Create a nested sketch block.

Nested sketch blocks convert into subassemblies when components are made from the layout. In this task, you will create a nested sketch block that represents the cylinder subassembly. It will consist of the **Cylinder Piston Rod** and **Cylinder Housing**.

1. In the Layout panel, click ![Create Block icon] (Create Block).

2. Select the Cylinder Piston Rod and Cylinder Housing sketch blocks.

3. Type **Cylinder** as the name and click **OK**.

The second instance that is created is an associative copy of the original sketch blocks.

4. In the Model Browser, expand the **Blocks>Cylinder** node. A second instance of each sketch block has been generated and added to this node. The **Cylinder Piston Rod** and **Cylinder Housing** blocks have also been removed from the top level of the sketch node and a copy of the instances added to the **Sketch1>Cylinder** node.

5. Move the **Cylinder Piston Rod** sketch block. The **Cylinder Housing** sketch block also moves and the kinematic motion created using the collinear constraint in the last task is no longer possible. To apply kinematic motion to a nested sketch block, you must activate the **Flexible** option.

6. In the Model Browser, in the **Sketch1** node, right-click on the Cylinder sketch block and select **Flexible**.

7. Move the **Cylinder Piston Rod** sketch block. Note that it can now be dragged independently of the **Cylinder Housing**.

Task 5 - Create second instances of the upper and middle braces.

Multiple instances of the upper and middle braces are required. Rather than recreate the geometry used in the sketch blocks, you will create a second instance of each block.

1. In the Model Browser, press and hold the left mouse button on the **Middle Brace** sketch block in either the **Sketch** or **Blocks** nodes and drag it into the graphic window. A second instance of the **Middle Brace** sketch block is added to **Sketch1**.

2. Create a second instance of the **Upper Brace**. The sketch displays as shown in Figure 4–17.

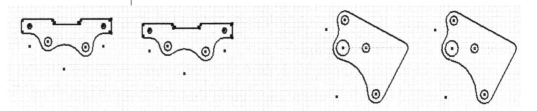

Figure 4–17

Task 6 - Modify the Middle Brace sketch block.

1. Another circle must be created on the **Middle Brace** sketch block to represent a hole that should be present in the 3D component. Click (Circle) to create a 25 mm diameter circle in one of the **Middle Brace** sketch blocks and constrain it as shown in Figure 4–18.

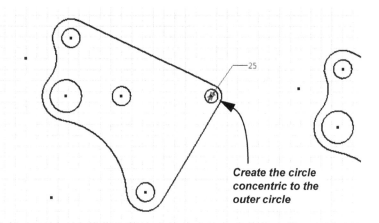

Create the circle concentric to the outer circle

Figure 4–18

2. The circle is not automatically added to the second instance of the **Middle Brace** sketch block. This is because the sketch block was not active when the circle was created.

   Double-click on the **Middle Brace** sketch block in which you created the circle to activate it. All other sketch blocks will dim. Ensure that the sketch block remaining in color is the one you have constrained the circle to. Once the sketch block is active, all dimensions associated with the sketch block re-display on the screen and the newly created circle displays gray.

3. Select the circle you just created. Right-click and select **Add To Block**. The circle is added to both instances of the sketch block and the circle is now black.

Task 7 - Constrain the upper braces to the Top Arm.

In this task, you will constrain the **Upper Braces** to the **Top Arm** sketch block. To do this, you will use coincident constraints. Because the holes of all three sketch blocks line up, it is difficult to create the constraints without first rotating the **Upper Brace** sketch blocks.

1. In the Model Browser, double-click on **Sketch1** reactivate it.

2. Select one of the **Upper Brace** sketch blocks.

3. In the Modify panel, click ⟳ (Rotate).

4. Click ▣ (Select) in the *Center Point* area in the Rotate dialog box. Select the center point of the small circle on the left side of the geometry, as shown in Figure 4–19.

5. Rotate the sketch block, as shown in Figure 4–19.

Rotate about the center point of this circle

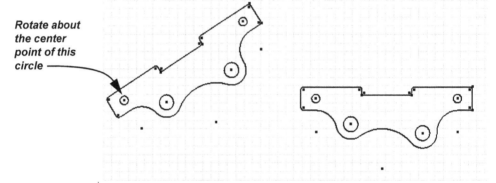

Figure 4–19

6. Rotate the other instance of the **Upper Brace** sketch block. The angle does not matter. The **Upper Brace** sketch blocks display approximately as shown in Figure 4–20.

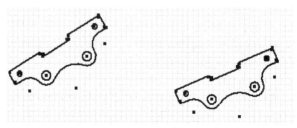

Figure 4–20

7. Using coincident constraints, constrain the center points of the two small holes in the **Top Arm** to the center points of the two small circles in one instance of the **Upper Brace** sketch block, as shown in Figure 4–21.

8. Constrain the other instance of the **Upper Brace** sketch block to the same location, as shown in Figure 4–21. For clarity, clear the Visibility of the first **Upper Brace** that was constrained while constraining the second instance. Resume its visibility when the second instance has been constrained.

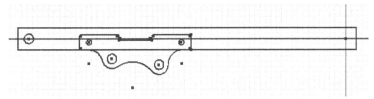

Figure 4–21

Task 8 - Constrain the middle braces together.

In this task, you will constrain the **Middle Braces** to each other. To do this, you will use coincident constraints. Because the holes of the sketch blocks line up, it is difficult to create the constraints without first rotating the **Upper Brace** sketch blocks.

1. Ensure that **Sketch1** is active.

2. Use the **Rotate** command to rotate one of the **Middle Brace** sketch blocks, as shown in Figure 4–22.

3. Apply coincident constraints on any of the two circle center points to align the two braces directly on top of each other. The result is shown in the right in Figure 4–22.

1. Rotate one of the Middle Brace sketch blocks

2. Apply coincident constraints between center points

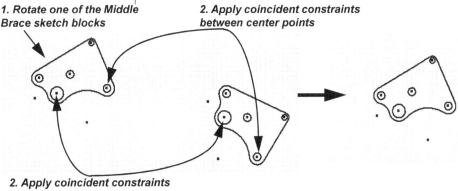

2. Apply coincident constraints between center points

Figure 4–22

Task 9 - Create additional geometry in the Top Arm sketch block.

In this task, you will create another circle in the **Top Arm** sketch block. The circle represents a hole in the 3D geometry.

1. In the Model Browser, double-click on **Top Arm** to activate it.

2. Create a 35mm diameter circle, as shown in Figure 4–23.

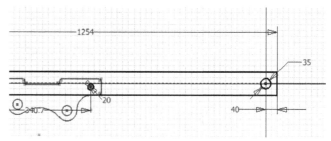

Figure 4–23

3. Right-click and select **Finish Edit Block**. When you create the additional geometry this time, it is automatically added to the sketch block.

Task 10 - Constrain the layout.

1. Activate **Sketch1**, if not already active.

2. Use coincident constraints between the center points of the circles to constrain the sketch blocks, as shown in Figure 4–24.

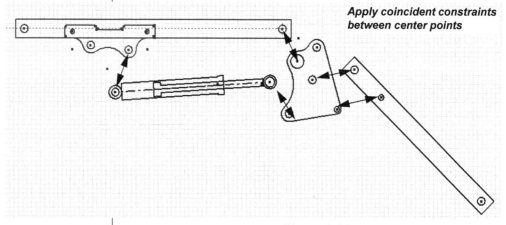

Apply coincident constraints between center points

Figure 4–24

3. Drag the center point of the connection between the **Cylinder Piston Rod** and the **Middle Brace** sketch blocks, as shown in Figure 4–25, to view the kinematic motion of the layout.

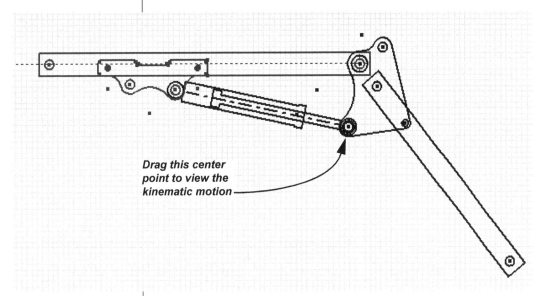

Drag this center
point to view the
kinematic motion

Figure 4–25

4. Finish the sketch and save the part file.

Task 11 - Generate components from the sketch blocks.

In this task, you will generate the required components from the sketch block. Components can be generated using two different commands: **Make Part** and **Make Components**. Because you want to create many components, it will be more efficient to create them using the **Make Components** command.

1. In the *Manage* tab>Layout panel, click ⊞ (Make Components).

2. In the Model Browser, expand the **Blocks** node and select all sketch blocks listed in the tree. The Make Components: Selection dialog box updates.

3. Leave the *Target assembly name* and *location* fields at the defaults.

4. Click 🗋 to open the Open Template dialog box.

Alternatively, you can pre-select all the blocks in the Model Browser, right-click and select ***Make Components***.

5. In the *Metric* tab, select the **Standard (mm).iam** template and click **OK**. The *Template* field updates, as shown in Figure 4–26.

Figure 4–26

6. Click **Next** to open the Make Components: Blocks dialog box.

7. Ensure that the Metric template is used for each component that will be generated. Select the first row in the dialog box and click ⬚. The Open Template dialog box opens.

8. In the *Metric* tab, specify the **Standard (mm).ipt** template and click **OK**.

9. Specify the **Standard (mm)** template for the remaining components. The Make Components: Blocks dialog box updates as shown in Figure 4–27. Select the **Standard (mm).iam** template for the Cylinder subassembly.

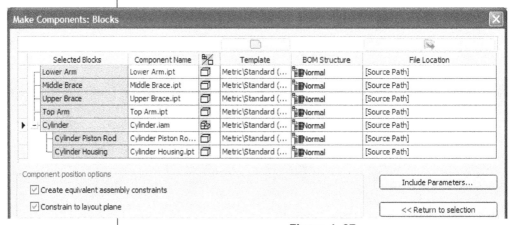

Figure 4–27

10. Leave all other options at their defaults and click **OK** to generate the assembly.

11. Review the Model Browser. Note the following:

    - Each sketch block has generated a separate component in the assembly, and the nested sketch block has generated a subassembly.
    - The first component in the assembly is a hidden grounded component. The component is the layout part.
    - Constraints have been created between the components. These constraints are based on the sketch constraints you created in the layout.

12. Expand the **Layout** node of the **Lower Arm** component. There are three flush constraints and one Z Angle constraint. These constraints are used to position the component in the assembly. Depending on the additional constraints used to position the component, these constraints are active or suppressed accordingly.

13. Expand other nodes in the Model Browser to view the other created constraints, as shown in Figure 4–28.

Figure 4–28

14. Save the assembly.

Task 12 - Make a design change in the layout.

In this task, you will make a design change. You will increase the length of the Lower Arm. After this change, you will return to the assembly and observe the effect.

1. Activate the **Layout.ipt** window.

2. Edit **Sketch1** and double-click on **Lower Arm** to activate the Lower Arm sketch block.

3. Change the *890 mm* dimension to **1000 mm**.

4. Finish editing the block and the sketch.

5. Return to the assembly window. Note that (Local Update) in the Quick Access Toolbar is active. Click

   (Local Update) to update the assembly. The length of the Lower Arm increases according to the change in the layout.

Task 13 - Create solid features.

In this task, you will create solid features from the sketch blocks. You will also offset some features away from the layout plane, so that they are correctly positioned in the assembly.

1. In the Assembly window, activate the **Lower Arm** component.

2. In the *3D Model* tab>Create panel, click (Extrude).

3. Create an extrude using the **Lower Arm** sketch block as the profile. Create it with a total distance of **80mm** and extrude it symmetrically about the sketch plane in both directions.

4. Activate the **Middle Brace:1** component.

5. Create an extrude using the **Middle Brace** sketch block as the profile. Extrude it to a **10mm** distance in the default direction. The model displays as shown in Figure 4–29.

Figure 4–29

The two **Middle Brace** components are not in the correct location. They need to be offset from the layout plane so that they are on either side of the **Lower Arm** component.

6. Activate the top-level assembly.

7. In the Model Browser, expand the **Middle Brace:1>Layout** node.

8. Select the XY Flush constraint. In the Model Browser, enter an offset of **40mm**.

9. Change the *XY Flush* offset for the **Middle Brace:2** component to **-50mm**. The assembly displays as shown in Figure 4–30.

Figure 4–30

Task 14 - (Optional) Complete the assembly.

Complete the assembly by building solid geometry for each of the remaining components and offsetting the **Upper Brace** components away from the Layout plane. The completed assembly displays as shown in Figure 4–31.

1. Consider the following:

*   Use extrudes and revolves when creating the geometry in the components.

*   Remember to make **Sketch1** visible again when required, for more than one feature in a component.

*   The blocks used in a layout will not always contain all the detail required to create the geometry. To create the cutout in the center of the Cylinder Housing, you need to edit **Sketch1** or create a new sketch to create the required geometry.

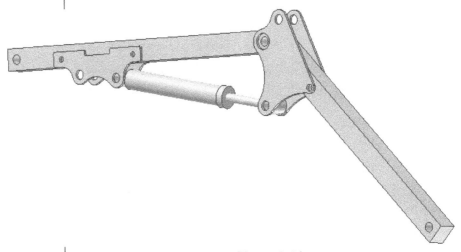

Figure 4–31

2. Save and close all open files.

Chapter Review Questions

1. Which of the following statements are true about creating a layout.

   a. When creating a layout in an assembly model, create a sketch at the top level assembly and create the required sketch blocks in the sketch.

   b. When creating a layout in a part model, create a sketch and create the required sketch blocks in the sketch.

   c. Both of the above.

2. Which of the following can be contained in a layout? (Select all that apply.)

   a. 2D entities

   b. 3D geometry

   c. Dimensions

   d. Constraints

3. When sketch blocks are nested, you are no longer able to test the kinematic motion of a model. Going forward, the nested blocks can only work as one component.

   a. True

   b. False

4. By default, all of the constraints created between sketch blocks are translated into assembly constraints. If you do not want to generate the assembly constraints, what do you need to do?

   a. Clear the **Constrain to layout plane** option when creating the components.

   b. Clear the **Create equivalent assembly constraints** option when creating the components.

   c. Delete them all after they are created.

   d. Clear the constraints individually from the Make Components dialog box.

5. How do you add another instance of a sketch block to a layout? (Select all that apply.)

   a. In the **Blocks** node, select the existing sketch block and drag it into the sketch.

   b. In the **Sketch** node, select the existing sketch block and drag it into the sketch.

   c. Right-click on the existing sketch block in the **Blocks** node and select **Copy** and then **Paste**.

   d. You can only have a single instance of a sketch block in a layout.

6. Components created from sketch blocks in a layout are associative to the layout.

   a. True

   b. False

Answers: 1.b, 2.(a,c,d), 3.b, 4.b, 5.(a,b), 6.a

Command Summary

Button	Command	Location
	Create Block	• **Ribbon**: *Sketch* contextual tab> Layout panel
	Make Components	• **Ribbon**: *Sketch* contextual tab> Layout panel
	Make Layout	• **Ribbon**: *Assemble* tab>Component panel
	Make Part	• **Ribbon**: *Sketch* contextual tab> Layout panel

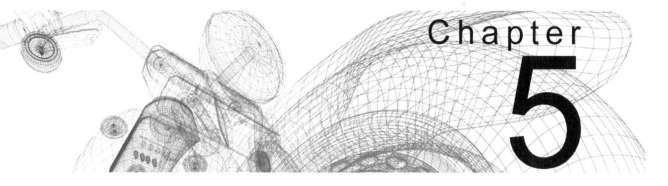

Chapter 5

Associative Links and Adaptive Parts

Associative links are automatically created in a model when you reference another component in an assembly to create geometry, dimensions, or constraints. When an associative link is established, the model is automatically set as adaptive. If an explicit associative link does not exist, you can still manually set a model (or a sketch-based feature in a model) to be adaptive.

Learning Objectives in this Chapter

- Break the associative link between a sketched feature and reference geometry.
- Specify geometric entities of part features to change, while controlling the size or location of other entities in an assembly.
- Ensure that a model remains as initially required by disabling unwanted adaptivity.

5.1 Associative Links

Each time you reference geometry (i.e., project geometry, dimensions to edges or faces on other components) to create a section of a new sketched feature, an associative link is applied between the reference geometry and the sketched feature, as shown in Figure 5–1.

By default, you can select references in the assembly for use in a new part. Using the Application Options dialog box, select the Assembly tab and clear the **Enable associative edge/loop geometry projection during in-place modeling** *option.*

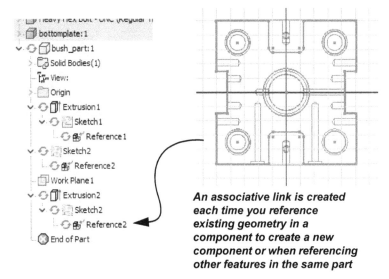

An associative link is created each time you reference existing geometry in a component to create a new component or when referencing other features in the same part

Figure 5–1

- Associative links automatically make the sketch *adaptive*.

- Adaptive features/parts are identified with ⟳ in the Model Browser. This means you cannot modify the referenced portions of the sketch because they are being adapted from some other reference in the assembly.

- Changes to the referenced geometry propagates to the associated (adaptive) geometry and it automatically updates, even if it impacts multiple parts.

Breaking Links

How To: Break the Associative Link Between a Sketched Feature and Reference Geometry

1. Edit or open the part that contains the feature in the assembly.
2. Expand the feature that you want to make independent and expand the reference sketch below it. The associative links are listed below the sketch.
3. Right-click on a reference link and select **Break Link**, as shown in Figure 5–2.

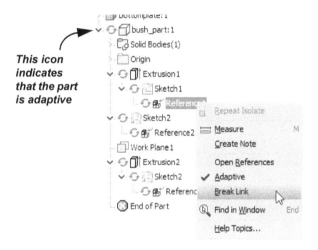

This icon indicates that the part is adaptive

Figure 5–2

Break each link individually to make the entire part independent.

Once the link is broken:

• The reference no longer displays in the Model Browser.

• Edit the feature and add any missing dimensions or constraints that are required.

Although references in the model are broken, it still indicates that the part and its features are adaptive. The fact that the features are still adaptive simply means that they are able to adapt if references to other geometry are added later in the design or are forced with assembly constraints. You can manually disable adaptivity so that unconstrained geometry does not update.

5.2 Adaptive Assembly Parts

The size and shape of a part might evolve as you put an assembly together. Rather than switch frequently between several files to edit the parts separately, you can use adaptivity. This enables you to specify geometric entities of part features to change, while controlling the size or location of other entities in an assembly. When you edit an adaptive part in the assembly, the adaptive components update accordingly.

Adaptive parts are recommended in the following situations:

- In the early stages of the design cycle, when some aspects of the design are prone to change. Adaptive parts are valuable because they adapt to change.

- In cases where a part or subassembly position is not defined.

- In cases where the size of a feature is dependent on another part.

The following unconstrained geometry can be made adaptive:

- Undimensioned sketch geometry

- Features based on undimensioned sketch geometry

- Work features based on geometry of other parts

- Parts containing adaptive sketches or features

- Subassemblies containing parts with adaptive sketches or features

When associative links are created in a component (parts, subassemblies, or features), the ⟳ icon automatically displays, as shown in Figure 5–3. You can also manually enable adaptivity so that unconstrained geometry updates. To do so, right-click on the component in the Model Browser and select **Adaptive**.

Figure 5–3

- The size of an adaptive element can be determined by the constraints used to locate the component in the assembly. For example, the size of the adaptive side component in the assembly shown on the left in Figure 5–4 is determined by constraining it to the box component.

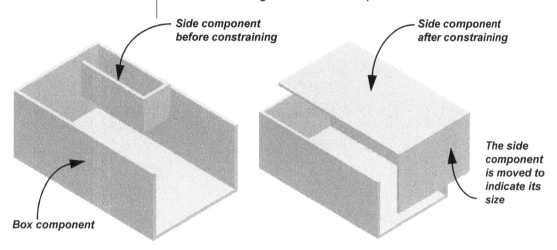

Side component before constraining

Side component after constraining

The side component is moved to indicate its size

Box component

Figure 5–4

Disabling Adaptivity

Breaking links does not automatically disable adaptivity. To disable adaptivity, right-click on the component's name in the Model Browser and clear the checkmark next to **Adaptive**. This is good design practice to ensure that if references are created unintentionally, the model remains as initially required. You can also remove adaptivity for specific features in the model instead of limiting it for the entire model.

Notes on Adaptivity

Keep the following considerations in mind when defining adaptive features:

- If a sketch is adaptive, only undimensioned and unconstrained geometry changes.

- Adaptive features can be modified by changing either their size, location, or both.

- If you use multiple instances of an adaptive element in an assembly, only one instance defines the adaptive features. All other instances are defined based on that instance. You might have to update twice to update all instances of adaptive elements.

- For a part to change size when other parts in the design change, the following must be adaptive: the part (in the context of the assembly), the feature (in the model), and the sketch of that feature.

- An assembly might have multiple adaptive parts, a part might have multiple adaptive features, and a feature might have multiple adaptive parameters.

- If an adaptive part is used in multiple assemblies, it can only be adaptive in one assembly.

- To make assemblies that contain adaptive parts update correctly, do not apply Mate constraints using points or between a line and a plane.

Practice 5a | Breaking Associative Links

Practice Objective

- Modify a component to make it independent by breaking its associative link to an assembly.

In this practice, you will break the associative links between the **bush_part** feature and its referenced geometry. In breaking these links, you will make the component independent.

Task 1 - Open an assembly file.

1. Open **Final Mold Assy2.iam** from the *Breaking Links* folder.

2. Toggle off the display of all assembly components, except for the **topplate2 Assy**, **Middleplate Assy**, and **bush_part** components.

3. Activate and expand the **bush_part** model. The associative links are listed below the sketch, as shown in Figure 5–5.

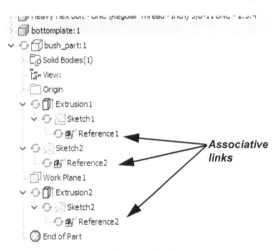

Figure 5–5

Task 2 - Modify the assembly and review how the model updates.

1. Leave the assembly open and open **bush_part** in a separate window. You will be toggling between the two windows throughout the remainder of the practice.

2. Return to the assembly window and activate the top-level assembly.

3. Right-click on the **Hole** that was created as the assembly feature and select **Edit Feature**.

4. In the Hole dialog box that opens, modify the diameter of the hole from *31.75* to **25**.

5. Activate the **bush_part** window. The model automatically updates to reflect the change in the diameter of the hole, as shown in Figure 5–6. This is because the hole was used as a reference in creating the outer diameter of the **bush_part**.

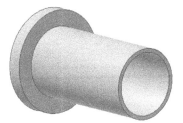

Figure 5–6

6. Return to the assembly window and change the diameter of the hole back to **31.75** mm. Note that the part updates.

7. In the assembly, in the Model Browser, right-click on **bush_part** and select **Adaptive** to clear the ability of this model to update with changes to any of its parent references.

8. Once again, modify the diameter of the hole from *31.75* to **25**.

9. Activate the **bush_part** window. The model does not update because all adaptivity for this component was disabled.

10. Return to the assembly window and change the diameter of the hole back to **31.75** mm.

11. Right-click on **bush_part** and select **Adaptive** to toggle adaptivity back on for the component. You should once again see ↻ beside the **bush_part** in the Model Browser.

You can disable adaptivity for specific features in the model instead of limiting it for the entire model. In this model, for example, you could clear the adaptivity for **Extrusion1**, while at the same time leaving **Extrusion2** adaptive, as shown in Figure 5–7.

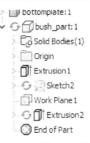

Figure 5–7

Task 3 - Break links between the part and the assembly.

As an alternative to disabling adaptivity, you can break the links that were generated when you created a model. Breaking links is permanent. Therefore, it should only be done if you know that you no longer want the relationship between the component and its parent.

1. Right-click on **Reference1** in the **bush_part** component and select **Break Link**. The reference no longer displays once you break the link.

2. Break the **Reference2** link. This can be done in either location, as it is a shared sketch.

3. Modify the diameter of the hole from *31.75* to **25** to test that the reference is no longer present.

Although the model still shows it is adaptive, no physical reference exists that could cause it to update. The fact that the features are still adaptive simply means that they are able to adapt if references to other geometry are added.

4. Edit the **Extrusion2** feature and extrude the sketch a distance of **5.08mm** instead of using the front face of topplate as the reference. The model displays as shown in Figure 5–8.

Figure 5–8

5. Delete **Work Plane 1**. This was the plane that was originally created to determine the distance of **Extrusion2**. Now that you have entered a specific value, this reference is not required.

6. Edit **Sketch1** and show all constraints. The geometry is fixed at a point. Add missing dimensions.

7. Save **bush_part** and close the window. Activate the assembly.

8. in the Model Browser, right-click on **bush_part** and select **Adaptive** to disable the link in the assembly model. The part is now independent and can be made adaptive in other assemblies.

9. Pattern **bush_part**. The model displays as shown in Figure 5–9.

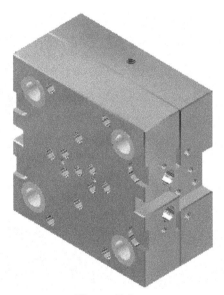

Figure 5–9

10. Save the assembly and close the window.

Practice 5b

Adaptive Assembly

Practice Objective

*   Enable a part in an assembly to update based on adaptivity in conjunction with assembly constraints.

In this practice, you will add a part to an assembly and set it so that it can update based on constraints set in the assembly. The resulting assembly is shown on the right in Figure 5–10.

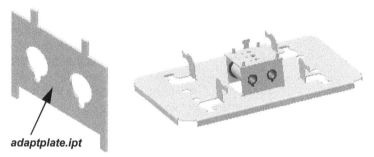

adaptplate.ipt

Figure 5–10

Task 1 - Open an assembly file.

1. Open **adapt.iam** from the top-level folder. The model displays as shown in Figure 5–11.

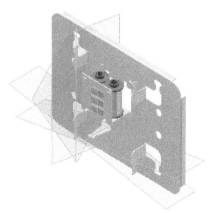

Figure 5–11

2. Toggle off all visible work features and **Component Pattern 1**.

3. Place one instance of **adaptplate.ipt** in the assembly.

4. Open **adaptplate.ipt** in a separate window and use the Model Browser options to examine the part. Note that no Adaptive features are in the model.

5. Close the **adaptplate.ipt** window.

Task 2 - Apply constraints to the assembly.

In this task, you will constrain the **adaptplate** part to the assembly to locate and adjust its size.

1. Apply Mate constraints between the center line of each coil and the center line of its corresponding large hole in the adaptplate. Apply another Mate constraint, offset **0.0135** between the large face of adaptplate and the face of the slot in the doorbellbase to locate the plate correctly, as shown in Figure 5–12.

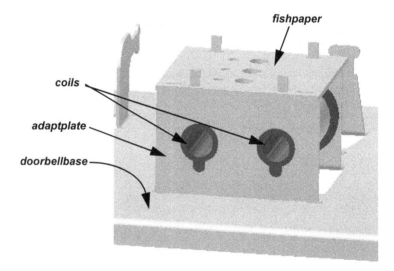

Figure 5–12

2. Examine the assembly. Note that the tabs at the top of **adaptplate** are not aligned with the slots in the small flat part (fishpaper).

3. in the Model Browser, right-click on **adaptplate** and select **Adaptive** to enable the part to change in the assembly.

   ↻ (Adaptive) displays beside the part icon in the Model Browser.

4. Apply a Mate constraint between the narrow surface on the **adaptplate** tab (that passes through the fishpaper) and the narrow surface of the slot in the fishpaper, as shown in Figure 5–13. Set the *Offset* to **0.025in** and apply the constraint. An error occurs, indicating that a constraint is inconsistent with another constraint and one of them must be edited, deleted, or suppressed. This is because the feature in the adaptplate is not set to be adaptive.

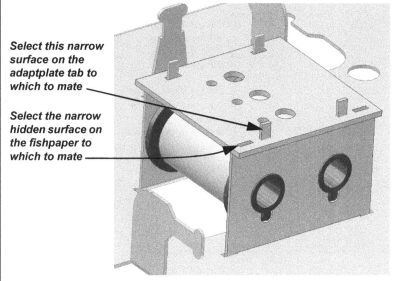

Select this narrow surface on the adaptplate tab to which to mate

Select the narrow hidden surface on the fishpaper to which to mate

Figure 5–13

5. Cancel the constraint placement and close the Place Constraints dialog box.

6. Open **adaptplate.ipt** in a separate window. The feature that must be set to adaptive is **Extrusion1** and its sketch. In the Model Browser, right-click on **Extrusion1** and select **Adaptive**. Note that the **Adaptive** icons for **Extrusion1** and its sketch are added, as shown in Figure 5–14.

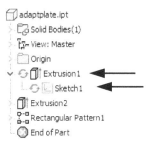

Figure 5–14

7. Return to the assembly window.

8. Once again, apply a Mate constraint between the narrow surface on the adaptplate tab (that passes through the fishpaper) and the narrow surface of the slot in the fishpaper, as shown in Figure 5–15. Set the offset to **0.025in** and apply the constraint. The tab adjusts to align with the slot because the extrusion in the adaptplate part was set to permit adaptivity.

Select this narrow surface on the adaptplate tab to which to mate

Select the narrow hidden surface on the fishpaper to which to mate

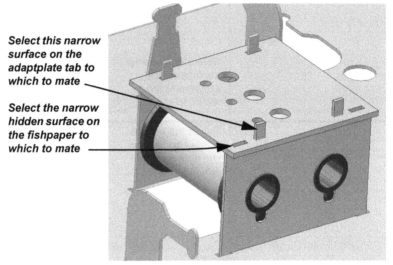

Figure 5–15

9. Add another Mate constraint and offset for the tab on the other side of adaptplate. The model displays as shown in Figure 5–16.

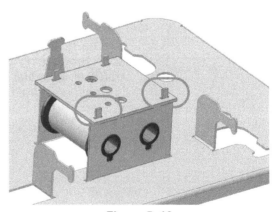

Figure 5–16

10. Save the assembly and parts and close the windows.

Chapter Review Questions

1. An associative link is created each time you reference existing geometry in a component to create a new component.

   a. True

   b. False

2. Which command is used to temporarily remove an associative link in a model.

   a. **Adaptive** (clear its selection)

   b. **Break Link**

3. Clearing adaptivity at the Part level of an assembly is the same as individually clearing adaptivity from all features in the part and leaving the part adaptive.

   a. True

   b. False

4. Which of the following are true regarding the Model Browser shown in Figure 5–17?

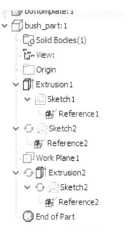

Figure 5–17

   a. The **bush_part:1** component in the assembly is adaptive.

   b. **Reference1** in the sketch for **Extrusion1** is adaptive.

   c. **Work Plane1** is adaptive.

   d. **Extrusion2** is adaptive.

5. Which of the following are valid statements about adaptivity of parts in an assembly? (Select all that apply.)

a. For a sketched feature in an assembly component to change size based on changes to other models, the part (in the assembly) and the feature and its sketch (in the part) must be marked as adaptive.

b. If a sketch is adaptive, entities that are fully constrained can be adapted from geometry in another component in an assembly.

c. Parts can be adaptive in multiple assemblies at one time.

d. Parts can have multiple adaptive features.

Answers: 1.a, 2.a, 3.b, 4.d, 5.(a,d)

Command Summary

Button	Command	Location
NA	Adaptive	• (context menu in the Model Browser)
NA	Break Link	• (context menu in the Model Browser)

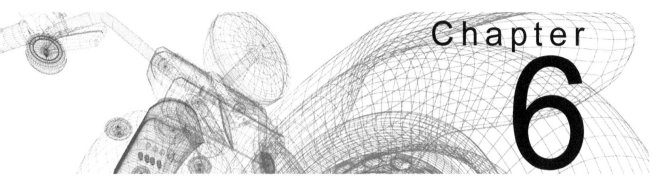

Chapter 6

Generative Shape Design

The Generative Shape Design tool available in the Autodesk® Inventor® software enables designers to set design criteria for a mass reduction target in a model. Based on assigned materials, constraints, and loads, the system returns a design suggestion that can be used to manipulate the model geometry to reduce its mass. Although this tool recommends a new shape, the manipulation is done manually using standard 3D modeling features. Once modified, stress analysis tools should be used on the model to ensure that it meets structural requirements.

Learning Objectives in this Chapter

- Create a Shape Generator study that sets a goal to meet a mass reduction target.
- Assign criteria in a Shape Generator study to accurately define a model's working environment.
- Promote a Shape Generator study to the modeling environment.

6.1 Shape Generator

The Shape Generator tool in Autodesk Inventor enables you to design light-weight models based on specified requirements. First, you must start with an Inventor model that approximates the overall volume or shape that is required. After setting the requirements and running the Shape Generator, you are presented with a 3D mesh design that you can use as a guide to redesign your initial geometry. Figure 6–1 shows the progression of a model from its initial design, through Shape Generator, to the final design.

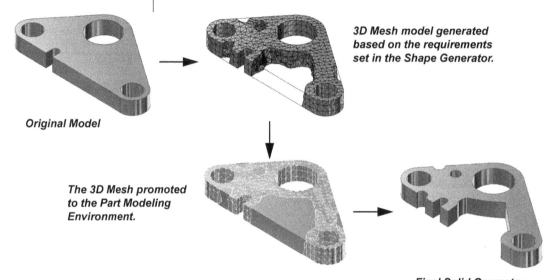

Original Model

3D Mesh model generated based on the requirements set in the Shape Generator.

The 3D Mesh promoted to the Part Modeling Environment.

Final Solid Geometry

Figure 6–1

How To: Generate a Design using Shape Generator

1. Open the model in the Shape Generator environment.
2. Define the material specification.
3. Apply constraints and loads that will represent the stresses that the part will encounter.
4. Define the Shape Generator Settings.
5. (Optional) Set zones that will be preserved during the analysis.
6. (Optional) Define symmetry in the model, if required.
7. Run the Shape Generator study.
8. Modify the initial design using the Shape Generator's 3D mesh as a guide for making modifications.

Preparing a Model for Shape Generator

Prior to initiating the Shape Generator tool, ensure that the Autodesk Inventor model represents the overall volume and shape of the intended geometry. The model should contain any required contact points (such as holes) that will represent pin locations and surfaces that will sustain forces.

> **Hint: Environment Support**
>
> Shape generator is only supported for single-body part modeling. It cannot be used for multi-body part or assembly design.

Opening Shape Generator

To open the Shape Generator environment, in the *3D Model* tab>Explore panel, click (Shape Generator). Click **OK** if prompted to review the learning tool. The *Analysis* tab opens as shown in Figure 6–2.

Figure 6–2

By default, a Shape Generator study is added to the Model browser once the *Analysis* tab is opened. The commands on this tab enable you to do the following:

- Create multiple shape generator analyzes and manage them.

- Assign material to an analysis.

- Assign constraints and loads to an analysis to define how the model is loaded in its working environment.

- Set goals and criteria for the analysis. This involves defining regions in the model that should not be changed as well as symmetry planes. Additionally, you set the criteria against which the design will be optimized. For example, reduce weight by x% to achieve a specific weight.

- Generate the optimized shape.

- Export the 3D mesh of the optimized shape to the modeling environment.

*While in the study, you can select **Modeling** at the top of the Model Browser to review the features in the design while remaining in the analysis.*

To create additional Shape Generator studies, in the Manage panel, click (Create Study), select **Shape Generator** in the Create New Study dialog box, and click **OK**.

> **Hint: Shape Generator in the Stress Analysis Environment**
>
> The Shape Generator functionality can also be accessed in the Stress Analysis environment. In the *3D Model* tab> Simulation panel, click (Stress Analysis). Once in the *Analysis* tab, click (Create Study), select **Shape Generator** in the Create New Study dialog box and click **OK**.

Material Assignment

In the Material panel, click (Assign) to open the Assign Materials dialog box, shown in Figure 6–3.

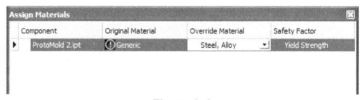

Component	Original Material	Override Material	Safety Factor
ProtoMold 2.ipt	Generic	Steel, Alloy	Yield Strength

Figure 6–3

- Maintain the **(As Defined)** option in the Override Material drop-down list to run the generator using the original material that was set in the modeling environment.

- Select an alternate material type in the Override Material drop-down list to study an alternative material.

- Select **Materials** to open and use the Material browser to define materials.

- Set the Safety Factor based on the **Yield Strength** or the **Ultimate Tensile Strength**.

- The material information is stored in the **Material** node for the active study. Each study that is setup in the Shape Generator environment can use a unique material setting.

Applying Constraints

You can assign constraints to the model to accurately define the translational or rotational degrees of freedom that exist in its working environment. **Fixed**, **Pin**, and **Frictionless** constraints can be assigned.

How To: Add Constraints

1. In the *Analysis* tab>Constraints panel, select the type of constraint to be assigned. Alternatively, you can right-click on the **Constraints** node in the Model browser and select the constraint type.

Constraint Type	Description
⤏I **(Fixed)**	Rmoves all degrees of freedom on a face, edge, or vertex.
◯ **(Pin)**	When used with cylindrical surfaces, it prevents faces from moving or deforming in combinations of radial, axial, or tangential directions.
▭ ⟷ **(Frictionless)**	When used with flat or cylindrical surfaces, it prevents the surface from moving or deforming in the normal direction relative to the surface.

2. In the applicable Constraint dialog box, select ⬚ (Location) and select the location to which the constraint is being assigned. Select faces, edges, or vertices, as required.

3. Click ⟩⟩ on the dialog box to access the additional constraint settings for each constraint type. The options in this portion of the dialog box enable you to further customize the constraint.

   - The **Display Glyph** option is used to enable/disable the visibility of the constraint glyph on the model.

   - A custom name can be assigned for the constraint, if required.

   - To apply a Fixed constraint with non-zero displacement, click **Use Vector Components** and enter X, Y, or Z values, as required.

   - For cylindrical surfaces, **Pin** constraints can be fixed radially, axially, or tangentially, as required. The default is to be fixed radially and axially.

4. Click **OK** to assign and close the dialog box. Alternatively, click **Apply** to assign the constraint and continue adding additional constraints of the same type.

Once added to the model, constraints are listed in the **Constraints** node in the Model browser. To edit them, right-click on the constraint name and select **Edit <Constraint Type>**.

Applying Loads

To accurately determine a shape using shape generator, you can assign loads that represent the applied load on the model. **Force**, **Pressure**, **Bearing**, **Moment**, **Gravity**, **Remote Force**, and **Body** loads can be assigned.

How To: Add Loads

1. In the *Analysis* tab>Loads panel, select the type of load to be assigned. Alternatively, you can right-click on the **Loads** node in the Model browser and select the load type.

Load Type	Description
(Force)	Assigns a force to a face, edge, or vertex. The force points to the inside of the part. You can assign the direction reference planar to a face or along a straight edge or axes.
(Pressure)	Assigns a pressure load to a face. Pressure is uniform and acts normal to the surface at all locations on the surface.
(Bearing)	Assigns a bearing load to a cylindrical face. By default, the load is along the axis of the cylinder and the direction of the load is radial.
(Moment)	Assigns a moment load to a face. You can assign the direction reference using a planar face, or along a straight edge or axes. The moment is applied around the direction to the selected face.
(Gravity)	Assigns the gravity load normal to the selected face or parallel with the selected edge.
(Remote Force)	Assigns a force at a specific point outside or inside the model. This option is located in the expanded Loads panel.
(Body)	Assign linear acceleration or angular velocity and acceleration for the model using a planar or cylindrical face as the input. This option is located on the expanded Loads panel.

You can only apply one Body load per Shape Generator study.

2. In the applicable Load dialog box, select ⬚ and select the reference to which the load is being assigned. Select faces, edges, or vertices, as required.

    •   A glyph displays on the model indicating the direction in which the load is applied. To change the direction, click

        ⬚ in the *Direction* area and select an alternate reference or flip the direction.

3. Define the magnitude of the load.

    •   Click ⬚ for Force, Bearing, Moment, Gravity, Remote Force, and Body loads to assign the magnitude values using vector components.

4. Click ⬚ on the dialog box to access additional settings for each load type. The options in this portion of the dialog box enable you to further customize the load.

    •   The **Display Glyph** option can be enabled/disabled to control the load glyph display, as required.

    •   The scale and color of the glyph display can be modified.

    •   A custom name can be assigned for the load, if required.

5. Click **OK** to assign and close the dialog box. Alternatively, click **Apply** to assign the load and continue adding additional loads of the same type.

Once loads are added to the model they are listed in the **Loads** node in the Model browser. To edit them, right-click on the constraint name and select **Edit <Force Load>**.

Hint: Multiple Loads on a Face

Consider using the **Split** command to split a single face if the face experiences multiple loading situations.

Shape Generator Settings

The Shape Generator settings enable you to define the design criteria. To open the Shape Generator Settings dialog box (shown in Figure 6–4) click  (Shape Generator Settings). By default, the 3D mesh model will be generated to maximize stiffness; however, you can also define the following additional criteria:

- Reduce the mass by a specified percentage or reduce it to a specific value.

- Define a specific member size that must be maintained during 3D mesh creation. This helps ensure that the mesh does not generate a wall thicknesses that can not be manufactured or might fail structural testing.

- The *Mesh Resolution* area provides a slider and a *Value* field that can be used to set the mesh resolution. A finer setting results in a smoother, higher quality mesh; however, it requires increased run time.

Figure 6–4

Preserving Regions

In most models, there will be regions of the design that should not be removed when generating a suggested 3D mesh. For example, specific areas around bolt holes or other supporting features may need to be maintained to allow the model to function as required.

How To: Preserve an Area on the Model

1. In the Goals and Criteria panel, click 🔧 (Preserve Region).

2. In the Preserve Region dialog box, click 🔲 and select a face on the model. Based on the selection of the face, a default preserved region boundary will appear on the model.

   - If a planar face is selected, a bounding box displays around the face, as shown in Figure 6–5.

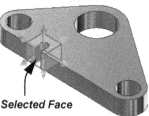

Figure 6–5

   - If a cylindrical face is selected, a bounding cylinder displays around the face, as shown in Figure 6–6.

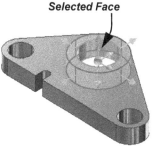

Figure 6–6

   - If the assumption of **Box** or **Cylinder** is not correct, you can switch the option in the *Region* drop-down list.

3. Refine the location and size of the bounding shape.

- Select **Move** and drag the center point of the displayed triad to reposition the bounding shape on the model.
- Select **Size** and activate and drag any of the handles that radiate from the bounding shape.
- Click >> to enter specific values for the center point and the bounding shape dimensions.

4. (Optional) In the expanded portion of the dialog box (>>) you can modify the glyph color, control its visibility, or enter a custom name for the preserved region.
5. Click **OK** to create the preserved region. Alternatively, click **Apply** to create the region and continue creating additional regions.

Once preserved regions are added to the model they are listed in the **Preserved Regions** node in the Model browser. To edit them, right-click on the constraint name and select **Edit Preserved Region**.

Assigning Symmetry

Symmetry planes can be assigned in the model to force the Shape Generator to produce a 3D mesh result that is symmetric about a selected plane or up to three planes (XY, XZ, or YZ).

How To: Assign Symmetry

1. In the Goals and Criteria panel, click ⊠ (Symmetry Plane).
2. By default, the symmetry planes are placed at the center of mass and are aligned with the global coordinate system. If required, use any of the following to modify the location of the default symmetry planes:

- To align the symmetry plane with a local UCS, click ⌖ (Local UCS) and select an active UCS. The symmetry plane is created in the local XY plane of the UCS.
- To place at the center of mass, click ⊕ (Center of mass). The UCS and symmetry plane are placed at the center of mass of the part.
- To place at the center of the bounding box of the part, click ⊹ (Center of bounding box). The UCS and symmetry plane are placed at the center of bounding box of the part.

3. Toggle the active planes ( ), as required, to define the model symmetry. Active planes appear red in the model.

4. (Optional) Click $\boxed{>>}$ to toggle the display of the symmetry glyph and assign a name for symmetry definition.

5. Click **OK** to close the dialog box. The symmetry Plane dialog box and a single symmetry plane are shown in Figure 6–7.

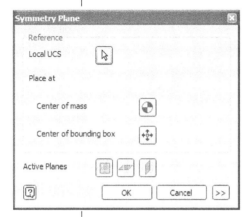

Figure 6–7

Once symmetry planes are added to the model, they are listed in the **Symmetry Planes** node in the Model browser. To edit them, right-click on the constraint name and select **Edit Symmetry Plane**.

Run the Shape Generator

The expandable area at the bottom of the dialog box reports warnings or errors while the process is being run.

Once the analysis has been setup, click (Generate Shape) to open the Generate Shape dialog box, as shown in Figure 6–8. Click **Run** to start the shape generator.

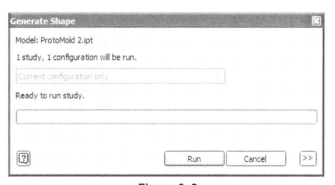

Figure 6–8

Once shape generation is complete, you are presented with a recommended 3D mesh model that can be used to guide your model design. Figure 6–9 shows the original model and a resultant mesh model after constraints, loads, and criteria were set.

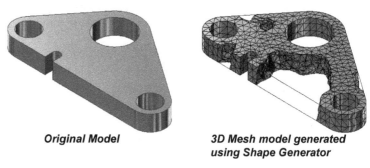

Original Model   *3D Mesh model generated using Shape Generator*

Figure 6–9

Promote the 3D Mesh Model

Once the mesh model has been generated, it can be promoted to the modeling environment to be used as a guide for making modeling changes to the geometry. In the Export panel, click

(Promote Shape) and select whether to copy the 3D mesh model directly to the part modeling environment (**Current Part File**) or to an STL file (**STL File**) that can be imported separately. Once the 3D mesh model is displayed, in the part modeling environment, you can use it as a guide to remove material from the part geometry.

Figure 6–10 shows an example of the promoted 3D mesh model in the part modeling environment and the final geometry based on suggested areas to be removed.

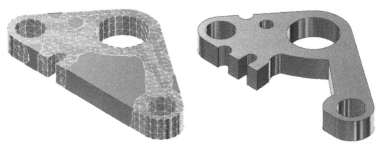

3D Model Promoted to the Part Modeling Environment   *Final Solid Geometry*

Figure 6–10

Consider the following when using a 3D mesh model to make changes to your design:

- When making geometry changes to the model, consider using lines and arcs where possible to help ensure that the final geometry is manufacturable.

- Not all geometry needs to be removed. This is a recommendation based on the criteria set.

The constraints and loads set in Shape Generator can be reused in the Stress Analysis environment.

- Consider using the Stress Analysis environment to further analyze the structural integrity of the final geometry.

Hint: Visual Style

Consider using the Wireframe visual style when using the 3D mesh model to make design changes. This enables you to see how the mesh model looks inside the solid geometry.

Practice 6a

Generating a Design using Shape Generator

Practice Objectives

- Create a Shape Generator study that sets a goal to meet a mass reduction target.
- Assign material, constraint, and load criteria in a Shape Generator study to accurately define a model's working environment.
- Set regions in the model that will not be removed after the Shape Generator study is complete.
- Define a symmetry plane in the model.
- Promote a Shape Generator study to the modeling environment.

In this practice, you will open a model that represents the overall shape and volume of an actuator mounting block that exists in a top-level assembly. The Shape Generator tool will be used to suggest modeling changes that helps to reduce the mass of the model to under 3 lbs. You will define the material, constraints, loads, preserved regions, and a symmetry plane prior to running the study. Figure 6–11 shows the model's progress through the practice.

  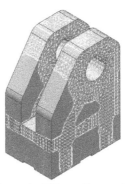 

Original Geometry *Analyzed 3D Mesh* *Promoted Shape Geometry* *Modified Solid Geometry*

Figure 6–11

Task 1 - Open an existing part model in the Shape Generator environment.

1. Open **Actuator Block.ipt** from the practice files folder.

2. In the *3D Model* tab> Explore panel, click (Shape Generator).

3. Click **OK** if prompted with the Shape Generator dialog box. This provides an introduction to the tool and the option to access Help documentation. If this was previously disabled, you will not be shown this dialog box.

4. The *Analysis* tab becomes the active tab and the model and Model browser display as shown in Figure 6–12. While in the study, you can select **Modeling** at the top of the Model Browser to review the features in the design while remaining in the analysis. The model is displayed in **Shaded with Hidden Edges** to better visualize the interior of the model. The overall shape of the model was created using the part modeling features.

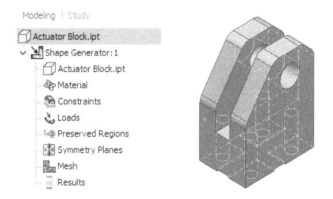

Figure 6–12

Task 2 - Define the material specification.

1. In the Material panel, click  (Assign) to open the Assign Materials dialog box, as shown in Figure 6–13.

Component	Original Material	Override Material	Safety Factor
Actuator Block_Final.ip	Steel AISI 1080	(As Defined)	Yield Strength

Figure 6–13

2. Maintain the **(As Defined)** option in the Override Material drop-down list. This uses the material that was defined when the model was created.

3. Click **OK**.

Task 3 - Apply constraints and loads that will represent the stresses that the part will encounter.

Pin constraints prevent faces from moving or deforming in combinations of radial, axial, or tangential directions

1. In the *Analysis* tab>Constraints panel, click 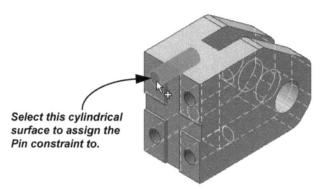 (Pin).

2. Ensure that the (Location) button is active and select the cylindrical surface shown in Figure 6–14.

Select this cylindrical surface to assign the Pin constraint to.

Figure 6–14

3. Click **Apply** to assign the constraint and leave the dialog box open. The Pin glyph displays on the model.

4. Continue to apply three additional Pin constraints to the remaining 3 support holes on the bottom of the model. Once assigned, the model and Model browser should display as shown in Figure 6–15.

A Pin constraint glyph displays on each support holes and the Constraints node is populated in the Model browser.

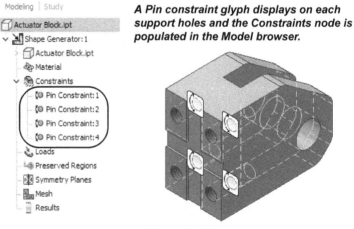

Figure 6–15

5. Click **Cancel** to close the dialog box.

6. Change the view display to **Shaded** if you had been working in an alternate view style.

7. In the *Analysis* tab>Loads panel, click 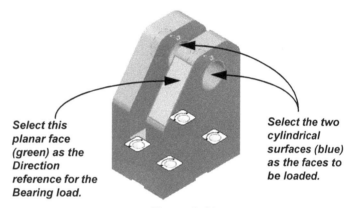 (Bearing).

8. Ensure that the (Faces) button is active and select the two cylindrical faces shown in Figure 6–16 as the reference faces to which the **Bearing** load is being assigned (blue faces).

9. By default, the load is along the axis of the cylinder and the direction of the load is radial. Click in the *Direction* area and select the face shown in Figure 6–16 as the direction reference (green face). A glyph displays on the model indicating the direction in which the load is applied.

To assign the load based on the vector directions, expand the dialog box and enter the values in the additional fields that are provided.

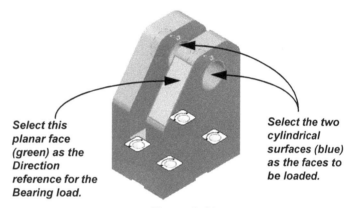

Select this planar face (green) as the Direction reference for the Bearing load.

Select the two cylindrical surfaces (blue) as the faces to be loaded.

Figure 6–16

10. Set the load *Magnitude* to **5000 N**, as shown in Figure 6–17.

Figure 6–17

11. Click on the dialog box to access the additional settings. Enter **Bearing** as the custom name for the load.

12. Click **OK** to assign the load and close the dialog box. The **Bearing** load has been added to the **Loads** node in the Model browser.

Task 4 - Define the Shape Generator Settings.

The current mass of the model is 4.51 Lbs. The design goal in this model is to reduce the weight to under 3 lbs.

1. To open the Shape Generator Settings dialog box, click
    (Shape Generator Settings).

2. Select **Target Mass** and enter **2.99lbmass**, as shown in Figure 6–18.

3. Maintain the *Mesh Resolution* slider at **3.000**, as shown in Figure 6–18.

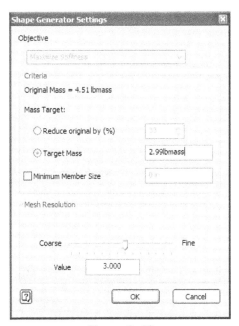

Figure 6–18

4. Click **OK**.

Task 5 - Set zones that will be preserved

1. In the Goals and Criteria panel, click (Preserve Region).

2. In the Preserve Region dialog box, click and select one of the cylindrical faces that was used in placing the **Bearing** load.

3. The Preserve Region dialog box updates to create a cylindrical region. Use the arrows on the various sides of the cylindrical bounding box to drag it, as shown in Figure 6–19. Ensure that the preserved area extends the width of the part and preserves the material above and around the holes.

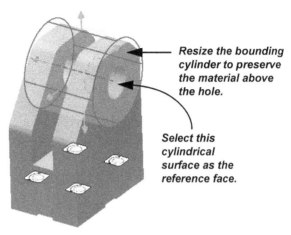

Resize the bounding cylinder to preserve the material above the hole.

Select this cylindrical surface as the reference face.

Figure 6–19

4. Click **OK**.

5. Reorient the model to the **BOTTOM** view using the ViewCube.

6. In the Model browser, expand the **Constraints** node. Right-click on **Pin Constraint1** and clear the **Visibility** option, as shown in Figure 6–20. This removes the glyph from the model display.

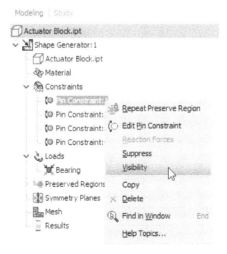

Figure 6–20

7. Clear the glyph display for the other three Pin constraints.

8. In the Goals and Criteria panel, click 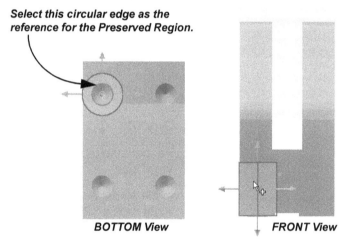 (Preserve Region).

9. Ensure that ⬚ is active and select the edge of the circular hole, as shown in the BOTTOM view in Figure 6–21.

10. Click `>>` to expand the dialog box. In the *Region Dimensions* area, set the *Radius* value to **0.4 in** and the *Length* value to **1.1 in**. Ensure that the length is extending into the model, as shown in the FRONT view in Figure 6–21. In the *Center Point* area, set the *Y* value to **.55in**.

Select this circular edge as the reference for the Preserved Region.

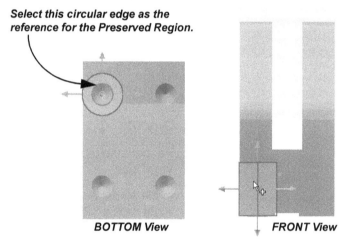

BOTTOM View　　　　　**FRONT View**

Figure 6–21

11. Create three identical preserved regions on the other support holes. The model should display as shown in Figure 6–22.

Figure 6–22

One additional preserve area is required to ensure that material is not removed that will affect the stability along the X axis.

12. Click 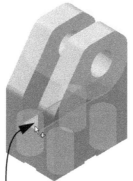 (Preserve Region), if the dialog box is not already open.

13. Select the planar face that connects the two symmetric sides. Using the ViewCube, reorient the model to size the bounding box similar to that shown in Figure 6–23. The box should extend the width of the model and extend into the preserve areas for the support holes. Click **OK** to create the preserved area.

Select this planar face to place the bounding box.   **Resize the bounding box to create this preserved area.**

Figure 6–23

14. All six preserved areas are listed in the **Preserved Regions** node in the Model browser.

Task 6 - Define symmetry in the model.

The model is symmetric about the YZ plane. This should be assigned as criteria to ensure that the 3D mesh model is symmetric.

1. In the Goals and Criteria panel, click (Symmetry Plane).

2. By default, the symmetry planes are placed at the center of mass and are aligned with the global coordinate system. No change is required to reposition the planes for this model.

3. Toggle the active planes so that the YZ plane is the only plane highlighted in red, as shown in Figure 6–24.

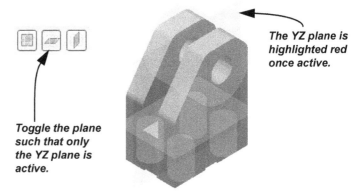

The YZ plane is highlighted red once active.

Toggle the plane such that only the YZ plane is active.

Figure 6–24

4. Click **OK** to assign the symmetry plane.

Task 7 - Run the Shape Generator and promote the study.

Now that the analysis has been setup, you can run the shape generator and promote the study to the model environment.

1. Click ⬚ (Generate Shape) to open the Generate Shape dialog box.

2. Click **Run** to start the shape generator analysis.

The analysis may take a few minutes to complete. The run time will vary depending on your computer.

Additionally, warnings may be presented as the geometry is optimized.

3. Once complete, a 3D mesh should be returned, similar to that shown in Figure 6–25.

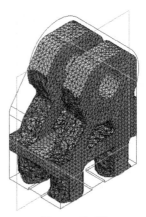

Figure 6–25

4. In the Export panel, click  (Promote Shape) and select **Current Part File** to promote the optimized 3D mesh directly to the part model. Click **OK**.

5. Click **OK** in the Promote Shape dialog box that displays. This dialog box, indicates that shape promotion was successful and provides recommended steps. The 3D mesh displays embedded in the solid geometry, as shown in Figure 6–26.

Figure 6–26

Task 8 - Modify the initial design using the Shape Generator's 3D mesh.

If time permits, try to create the sketches in your own model.

1. Open **Actuator Block_Final.ipt**. This model already has been optimized using Shape Generator and sketches that approximate the material removal have been created for you.

2. Using the **Side Cut Profiles** and **Front Cut Profile** sketches, create the geometry shown in Figure 6–27.

Figure 6–27

3. Open the model's iProperties dialog box and update its physical properties. Note that the mass is still slightly over 3lbs.

4. To further reduce the mass of the model, you can add fillets to the edges of the geometry, modify the sketches that were used to remove the material, and/or change to a lower weight steel. Ultimately, the changes that are made must still be analyzed for structural integrity to ensure it can withstand its loads; however, the Shape Generator has provided a satisfactory starting point.

5. Save the model and close the window.

Chapter Review Questions

1. The Shape Generator tool automatically modifies the initial geometry of the model when it is promoted to the part modeling environment.

    a. True

    b. False

2. In which Autodesk Inventor working environment can you gain access to the Shape Generator tool? (Select all that apply.)

    a. Part Modeling

    b. Assembly Modeling

    c. Drawing

    d. Presentation

    e. Stress Analysis

3. Only a single shape generation study can be setup in a model.

    a. True

    b. False

4. Which of the following constraints can be added to the model to accurately describe how it is constrained in its working environment? (Select all that apply.)

    a. **Bearing**

    b. **Fixed**

    c. **Force**

    d. **Frictionless**

    e. **Gravity**

    f. **Moment**

    g. **Pin**

    h. **Pressure**

5. Which of the following cannot be controlled using the additional options in the expandable load creation dialog boxes? (Select all that apply.)

   a. The location reference of the load.

   b. The direction reference for a load.

   c. The magnitude of the load broken down into vector components.

   d. The assignment of a custom load name.

   e. The display of the load glyph in the model.

   f. The scale of the load glyph when it is displayed in the model.

6. Which of the following are valid when setting the criteria for a Shape Generator analysis? (Select all that apply.)

   a. The volume of the model is set to reach a target value.

   b. The mass of the model is set to reach a target value.

   c. The volume of the model is reduced by a set percentage value.

   d. The mass of the model is reduced by a set percentage value.

7. A cylindrical face that is selected as the reference for a preserved region cannot use the **Box** option to define its boundary.

   a. True

   b. False

8. How many planes can be selected during a Shape Generator analysis to define symmetry in a model?

   a. 1

   b. 2

   c. 3

   d. Unlimited

Answers: 1.b, 2.(a,e), 3.b, 4.(b,d,g), 5.(a,b), 6.(a,d), 7.b, 8.c

Command Summary

Button	Command	Location
	Assign (material)	• **Ribbon:** *Analysis* tab>Material panel • **Context Menu:** In Model browser with Material node selected
	Bearing Load	• **Ribbon:** *Analysis* tab>Loads panel • **Context Menu:** In Model browser with Loads node selected
	Body Load	• **Ribbon:** *Analysis* tab>Loads panel • **Context Menu:** In Model browser with Loads node selected
	Create Study	• **Ribbon:** *Analysis* tab>Manage panel
	Finish Analysis	• **Ribbon:** *Analysis* tab>Exit panel
	Fixed Constraint	• **Ribbon:** *Analysis* tab>Constraints panel • **Context menu:** In Model browser with Constraints node selected • **Context menu:** In graphics window
	Force Load	• **Ribbon:** *Analysis* tab>Loads panel • **Context Menu:** In Model browser with Loads node selected • **Context menu:** In graphics window
	Frictionless Constraint	• **Ribbon:** *Analysis* tab>Constraints panel • **Context Menu:** In Model browser with Constraints node selected
	Generate Shape	• **Ribbon:** *Analysis* tab>Run panel • **Context Menu:** In Model browser with Study node selected
	Gravity Load	• **Ribbon:** *Analysis* tab>Loads panel • **Context Menu:** In Model browser with Loads node selected
	Mesh View	• **Ribbon:** *Analysis* tab>Mesh panel • **Context Menu:** In Model browser with Study node selected • **Context menu:** In graphics window
	Moment Load	• **Ribbon:** *Analysis* tab>Loads panel • **Context Menu:** In Model browser with Loads node selected
	Pin Constraint	• **Ribbon:** *Analysis* tab>Constraints panel • **Context Menu:** In Model browser with Constraints node selected
	Preserve Region	• **Ribbon:** *Analysis* tab>Goals and Criteria panel

	Pressure Load	• **Ribbon:** *Analysis* tab>Loads panel • **Context Menu:** In Model browser with Loads node selected
	Promote Shape	• **Ribbon:** *Analysis* tab>Export panel
	Remote Force Load	• **Ribbon:** *Analysis* tab>Loads panel • **Context Menu:** In Model browser with Loads node selected
	Shape Generator	• **Ribbon:** *3D Model* tab>Explore panel
	Shape Generator Settings	• **Ribbon:** *Analysis* tab>Goals and Criteria panel
	Stress Analysis	• **Ribbon:** *3D Model* tab>Simulation panel
	Symmetry Plane	• **Ribbon:** *Analysis* tab>Goals and Criteria panel

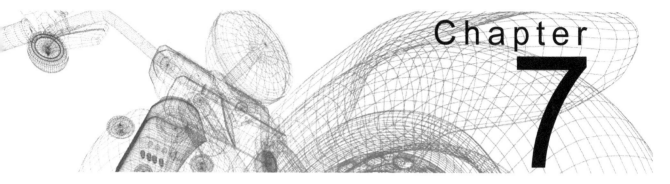

Frame Generator

Frame Generator enables you to quickly and easily create the members (parts) in a structural framework. The frame members that are created have predefined cross-sections in the Autodesk® Inventor® software. The frame members are generated based on 2D and 3D sketched geometry in a skeleton part model that is assembled into a top-level assembly.

Learning Objectives in this Chapter

- Quickly and easily create structural frames, using a skeletal wireframe part to define the location of structural frame members.
- Adjust frame member ends to obtain required joints.
- Create and publish custom frame member profiles to the Content Center.

7.1 Frame Generator

The Frame Generator quickly and easily creates structural frames, such as those used in machines, fixtures, platforms, access ways, and stairwells. To define the location of structural frame members, a skeletal wireframe part is used (consisting of 2D sketches, 3D sketches, edges, and vertices). An example of a structural frame with its generated members is shown in Figure 7–1. Any changes made to the skeletal wireframe part automatically update the associated frame members.

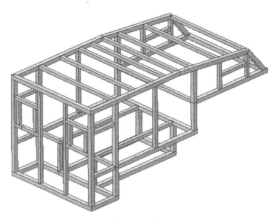

Figure 7–1

General Steps

Use the following general steps to add structural frame members:

1. Create a skeletal model.
2. Insert the skeletal model into an assembly.
3. Insert frame members.
4. Define the Frame Member Selection options.
5. Define the Placement method and reference(s).
6. Define the Orientation options.
7. Apply the frame member definition.
8. Insert additional members, as required.
9. Reuse members, as required.
10. Adjust frame member definition, as required.
11. Adjust frame member ends, as required.

Step 1 - Create a skeletal model.

Create a skeletal part model (using 2D and 3D sketches) to use as a reference for defining the location of the structural frame members. A sketch can contain linear entities, splines, construction lines and other entities. A sample skeletal model for a truck camper is shown in Figure 7–2.

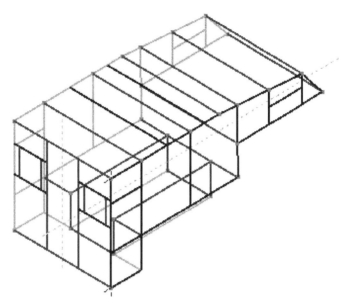

Figure 7–2

Step 2 - Insert the skeletal model into an assembly.

Create a new assembly or use an existing assembly and place the skeletal model in the assembly. Save the assembly.

Step 3 - Insert frame members.

In the *Design* tab>Frame panel, click 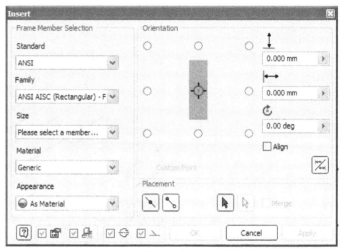 (Insert Frame). The Insert dialog box opens, as shown in Figure 7–3.

Figure 7–3

Select the entities in the skeletal model where you want to assign the frame members.

- Only select entities that have the same member properties.

- Enable ⊕ and ⅄ to enable you to select centerline and construction lines respectively.

Step 4 - Define the Frame Member Selection options.

Use the drop-down lists in the *Frame Member Selection* area to define the following options:

- Engineering standard (Standard drop-down list).

- Profile type (Family drop-down list)

- Size (Size drop-down list).

- Material style to apply (Material Style drop-down list).

- Appearance to apply (Appearance drop-down list). Use the **As Material** option to display the color style of the material.

Step 5 - Define the Placement method and reference(s).

There are two placement methods: **On Edges** and **Between Points**.

You cannot define frame member placement references using a combination of the ***On Edges*** *and* ***Between Points*** *methods.*

- Use (On Edges) to define the placement references by selecting edges of solid bodies, and lines, arcs, or splines from 2D and 3D sketches. Using this placement method, you can create multiple members at the same time using a window selection or right-clicking in the main window to change selection method to Multi Select, **Chain Select**, or **Sketch Select**.

If multiple members share the same end points, you can merge them by selecting the ***Merge Resulting Members*** *option in the Placement area.*

- Use (Between Points) to define the placement references by selecting a start and end point. Only a single member can be created at a time using this placement method.

In the *Placement* area, select the required method and then select the references from the model.

Step 6 - Define the Orientation options.

Use the *Orientation* area to define how the profile is inserted. The buttons locate the position of the profile with respect to the frame member placement reference (the edge, line, arc, or spline selected to define the location of the frame member).

in the *Orientation* area indicates where the frame member placement reference is located relative to the profile. For example, if the symbol displays in the center, as shown in Figure 7–4, the frame member placement reference is located at the center of the profile.

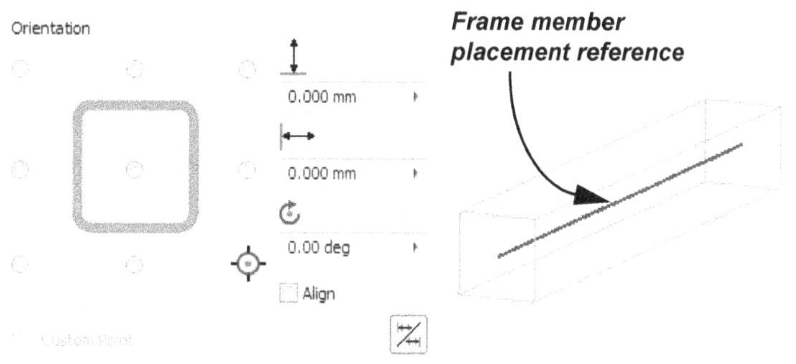

Figure 7–4

The additional options in the dialog box are described as follows:

Vertical Offset ↕ 0.000 mm ›	Defines a vertical offset distance to offset the profile from the frame member placement reference.
Horizontal Offset ↔ 0.000 mm ›	Defines a horizontal offset distance to offset the profile from the frame member placement reference.
Select or Input Angle ↻ 0.00 deg ›	Rotates the profile with respect to the frame member placement reference.
Mirror Frame Member	Mirrors the profile with respect to the frame member placement reference.
Prompt For File Name ☑ ☞	Prompts for each frame member file and display name once you have completed the frame member definition. You can copy and paste text.
Get Frame Member's Part Number from Content Center ☑ ⛭	Updates the part number to coincide with the Content Center. If cleared, the part number does not update, enabling you to enter a custom name.
Align	Enables you to select geometry to align frames instead of entering a rotation angle. You can select a planar face, view edge, work axis, work plane, or sketch line.

Step 7 - Apply the frame member definition.

Once the frame member is defined, click **Apply** or **OK** to insert the frame member into the model. Using the **Apply** option enables you to continue creating members once the first has

been created. If ☑ ☞ was selected, the Frame Member Naming dialog box opens for you to enter filenames. Click **OK** when finished entering the required names. A new part file is created for each frame member, even if some are identical.

Step 8 - Insert additional members, as required.

Define additional frame members, as required. Once finished inserting frame members, click **Cancel**.

Step 9 - Reuse members, as required.

To reduce the number of files that are created, you can reuse any members that are identical.

*The **Reuse** command is not available for curved members.*

How To: Reuse Identical Members

1. In the *Design* tab>Frame panel, click (Reuse). The Reuse dialog box opens, as shown in Figure 7–5.

Figure 7–5

2. Select an existing member that is to be reused. The selection can be made in the graphics window or in the Model Browser. Once selected, the member is identified in the *Source Member* area.

3. Select the (Insert Members on Edges) or (Insert Members between Points) placement type and select entities or points as required in the model to place the reused member.

   - The member can only be located on an identical placement reference. Only entities that produce an identical member are selectable.
   - To select multiple identical placement references at the same time, select them individually or drag a window around the model.

Hint: Member Selection

When selecting members to reuse, the selection location on the entity affects the orientation of the new member. The orientation can be edited once placed using the **Change Reuse** command.

4. By default, the Orientation settings are assumed to be the same as those used when the source member was added. However, the location of the selection can also affect the orientation. You can use the **Change Reuse** command to change the selection once it has been placed, if required.

5. Click **Apply** to add the new member and continue reusing the members in the model. Click **OK** to add the new member and close the dialog box.

Step 10 - Adjust frame member definition, as required.

Once frame members are inserted or are reused, there might be situations where they need to be edited.

Change

In the *Design* tab>Frame panel, click (Change) to change the definition of a inserted (parent) frame member. The Change dialog box presents the same options as the Insert dialog box.

To redefine multiple frame members at once, activate the **Multi-Select** option. To change the orientation of multiple frame members, select the **Change Orientation** option. Once you have finished redefining, click **Apply** to apply the changes and continue redefining additional frame members, or click **OK** to apply the changes and close the Change dialog box.

Change Reuse

The **Change Reuse** command edits the geometry reference that was selected when the member was initially reused, or the reference's positional orientation settings. In the Frame panel,

click (Change Reuse) to open the Change Reuse dialog box. Select the member that you want to change and change the settings as required.

- Click 🖉 (Reverse Member Direction) in the *Select* area to flip the direction of the member.

- Select new orientation positions for where the member should be located with respect to the reference entity.

- Enter a vertical offset, horizontal offset, or angular value to reposition the frame member from the selected reference entity.

Step 11 - Adjust frame member ends, as required.

Once the frame members are added, you might need to adjust the frame member ends by using one or more of the following options:

- **Trim To Frame**

- **Notch**

- **Lengthen - Shorten**

- **Miter**

- **Trim - Extend**

- **Remove End Treatments**

Hint: End Treatments for Reused Members

The end treatments that are used on members should be considered when deciding to reuse members. Any end treatment on a parent member is also applied to the reused member.

Trim To Frame

Trim To Frame trims or extends two frame members to one another. The first selected frame member (highlighted in blue) is trimmed or extended to the second intersecting face of the second selected frame member (highlighted in yellow). The second frame member is trimmed or extended up to the first intersecting face of the first frame member.

How To: Use the Trim To Face Option

1. In the *Design* tab>Frame panel, click 🖵 (Trim to Frame). The Trim to Frame dialog box opens.
2. Select the first frame member (blue) to be trimmed or extended to the second intersecting face of the second frame member (yellow).
3. Select the second frame member (yellow) to be trimmed or extended to the first intersecting face of the first frame member (blue).
4. (Optional) Define a vertical offset value for trimming.
   - Specify a positive value to extend the first frame member (blue) past the second intersecting face as shown on the left of Figure 7–6.
   - Specify a negative value to set the member back from the second intersecting face as shown on the right of Figure 7–6.

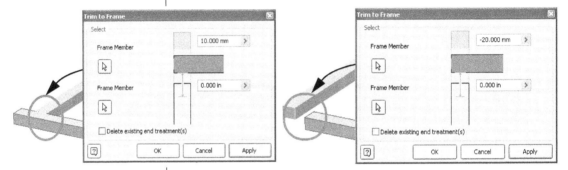

Figure 7–6

5. (Optional) Define a horizontal offset value for trimming.
   - A positive value sets back the second selected frame member (yellow) from the first intersecting face of the first selected frame member (blue) as shown on the left of Figure 7–7.
   - A negative value extends the second selected frame member (yellow) past the first intersecting face of the first selected frame member (blue) as shown on the right of Figure 7–7.

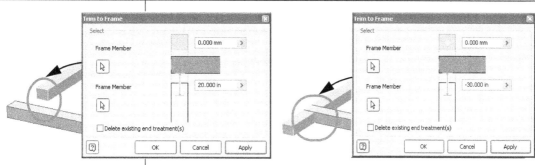

Figure 7–7

6. Click **Apply** to apply the trim. If the result needs to be modified, select the same references again and adjust the offset values, as required. Reapply the changes.
7. Perform the operation on other frame members, as required and click **OK** when finished.

Figure 7–8 and Figure 7–9 show examples of the references and the resulting trimmed members.

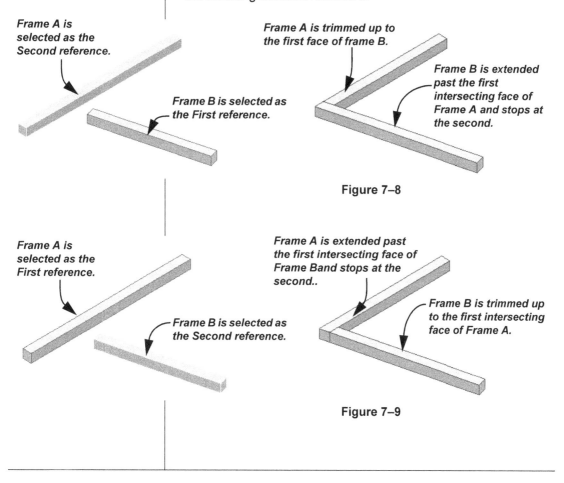

Frame A is selected as the Second reference.

Frame B is selected as the First reference.

Frame A is trimmed up to the first face of frame B.

Frame B is extended past the first intersecting face of Frame A and stops at the second.

Figure 7–8

Frame A is selected as the First reference.

Frame B is selected as the Second reference.

Frame A is extended past the first intersecting face of Frame Band stops at the second..

Frame B is trimmed up to the first intersecting face of Frame A.

Figure 7–9

- The **Trim To Frame** option can still be used if the two selected references do not lie on the same plane. The members are still trimmed and extended to the planar faces as if they existed on the same plane.

Notch

Use the **Notch** option to cut one frame member by using the shape or a custom notch profile on a second, as shown in Figure 7–10.

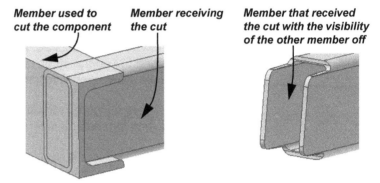

Member used to cut the component

Member receiving the cut

Member that received the cut with the visibility of the other member off

Figure 7–10

How To: Use the Notch Option

1. In the *Design* tab>Frame panel, click [icon] (Notch).
2. Select the frame member you want to cut.
3. Select the frame member to use as the cutting reference.
4. Click **Apply** to create the notch. You can continue creating additional notches or click **OK** to create the notch and close the Notch dialog box.
   - If the secondary frame member that is being used to create the notch was created and published as a notch profile, you have the option of enabling/disabling the use of the notch profile.

Lengthen - Shorten Frame Member

Use the **Lengthen /Shorten** command to increase or decrease the length of a frame member.

How To: Lengthen or Shorten a Frame Member

1. In the *Design* tab>Frame panel, click ⊞ (Lengthen/ Shorten). The Lengthen - Shorten Frame Member dialog box opens, as shown in Figure 7–11.

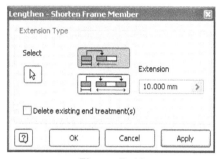

Figure 7–11

2. Select one of the following extension value placement methods:

   • Click ⊞ to increase or decrease the length of the selected frame member by the defined value, at one end.

   • Click ⊞ to increase or decrease the length of the selected frame member by the defined value, at both ends.

3. Select the frame member to lengthen. If ⊞ is the method, select nearest the end you want to extend.
4. Enter the required value in the *Extension* field. A positive value increases the length, a negative value decreases the length.
5. Click **Apply** to apply the **Lengthen** command and continue using the command or click **OK** to apply and close the dialog box.

Miter

Use the **Miter** option to cut the ends of two frame members at equal angles to form a corner, as shown on the right in Figure 7–12.

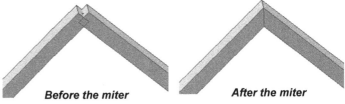

Before the miter　　　　**After the miter**

Figure 7–12

How To: Miter the Ends of Two Frame Members

1. In the *Design* tab>Frame panel, click ⌐ (Miter). The Miter dialog box opens, as shown in Figure 7–13.

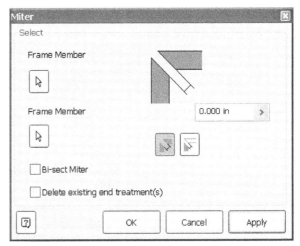

Figure 7–13

2. Select the type of miter.

   • Click 🔲 to miter with a gap equal to the defined value.

   • Click 🔲 to miter with a gap on the first selected frame member equal to the defined value. Figure 7–14 shows an example of a miter cut at one side.

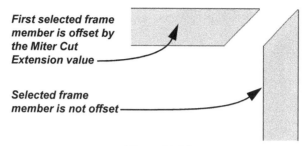

First selected frame member is offset by the Miter Cut Extension value

Selected frame member is not offset

Figure 7–14

3. Select the first and second frame members to miter. The selection order only matters if you selected the ⬚ miter type.
4. Enter a value in the *Miter Cut Extension* field, as required.
5. Click **Apply** to apply the miter and continue using the Miter command or click **OK** to apply the miter and close the Miter dialog box.

Trim - Extend To Face

Use **Trim/Extend** to trim or extend one or more frame members to a model face.

How To: Trim or Extend One or More Frame Members to a Face

1. In the *Design* tab>Frame panel, click ⬚ (Trim/Extend). The Trim - Extend To Face dialog box opens, as shown in Figure 7–15.

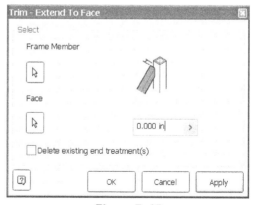

Figure 7–15

2. Select the frame members to trim or extend to a common face.

3. Click [⬚] and select the face to which the selected frame members are going to be trimmed or extended.

4. Enter an offset value, as required.

5. Click **Apply** to extend or trim the frame member(s) to the selected face and continue using **Trim - Extend To Face** or click **OK** to extend or trim the frame member(s) to the selected face and close the Trim-Extend To Face dialog box.

Remove End Treatments

Use **Remove End Treatments** to return a frame member to its original state of creation, before any modifications. Multiple frame members can be selected. To remove any end treatments to a member, click [⬚] (Remove End Treatments) in the *Design* tab>expanded Frame panel. Select the member(s) and complete the operation. This option is useful for returning to a previous version of the model when undo does not enable you to do so (e.g., when a model is opened in a new session).

Additional Options

- In the *Design* tab>expanded Frame panel, click [⬚] (Frame Member Info) to quickly obtain information about a frame member, as shown in Figure 7–16.

Figure 7–16

- Consider the use of the **Beam/Column Calculator** and **Plate Calculator**. These are both available in the *Design* tab>expanded Frame panel. The options in these calculators can be used to aid in creating a structurally sound assembly.

7.2 Structural Shape Author

Using the Structural Shape Author, you can publish custom profiles to the Content Center, similar to that shown in Figure 7–17.

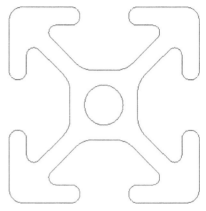

Figure 7–17

General Steps

Use the following general steps to use the Structural Shape Author to create a custom frame member:

1. Create a Read/Write library in the Content Center.
2. Prepare the structural shape and properties.
3. Author the structural shape.
4. Publish the structural shape.

Step 1 - Create a Read/Write library in the Content Center.

For more information about creating Content Center libraries and their configuration, see the Autodesk Inventor Help Topics and your local Administrative support.

Before you begin creating new structural shapes for use in the Frame Generator, you must create a Read/Write library in the Content Center and attach it to your project. Setting up the Content Center is a crucial step in the process of creating valid published shapes.

Step 2 - Prepare the structural shape and properties.

When creating a custom shape, consider how accurate the shape should be and how much detail to include. A frame profile that is very detailed might not be required and can slow down modeling. Consider critical dimensions carefully and include those that are required. Sketch, constrain, and dimension the profile using parameters and equations where useful. Complete the sketch and create a simple extrusion to accommodate the authoring process. The model in Figure 7–18 shows the dimension scheme (with equations) and the 3D extruded model that is required.

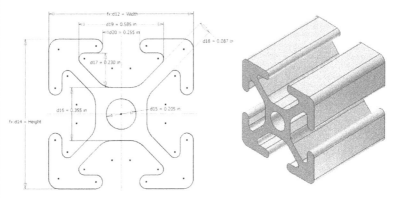

Figure 7–18

Ensure that you have the correct physical material for the new structural shape created in your templates or style library. The material should contain at least the correct value for density, but can also contain more information about the material's properties (such as Yield Strength [MPa], Ultimate Tensile Strength [MPa], and Young's Modulus [GPa]). Also consider the use of more complex parameters where possible (e.g., Section Area, Moment of Inertia for X and Y). These material properties and parameters are important for the **Beam and Column Calculator** in the Frame Generator and are mapped to corresponding items during the publishing process.

Step 3 - Author the structural shape.

The authoring process takes a basic extrusion and converts it to a valid Frame Generator profile using automatic feature modification. To open the Author, in the *Manage* tab>Author panel, click 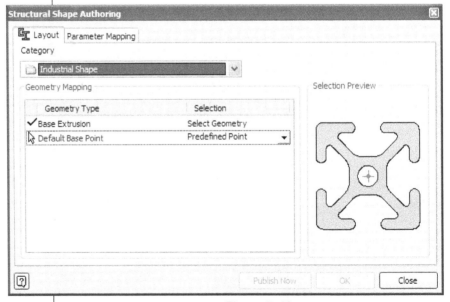 (Structural Shape Authoring) from the Component drop-down list.

The options available on the two tabs (*Layout* and *Parameter Mapping*) enable you to author the structural shape.

Layout

The *Layout* tab is shown in Figure 7–19, and described as follows:

*   Select the category in the Read/Write Content Center library where the shape should be populated.

*   The *Geometry Mapping* area automatically populates selected geometry (if there is only one extrusion in the part).

*   The Default Base Point is the geometric center of the profile. You can select a new Base Point from the menu, if required.

Figure 7–19

Parameter Mapping

The *Parameter Mapping* tab enables you to map the parameters
required in the Content Center to the parameters in the model.

The *Parameter Mapping* tab is shown in Figure 7–20. Click [...]
to specify an iProperty or parameter to map.

- Fields with a yellow background are required fields, while
  fields in white are optional.

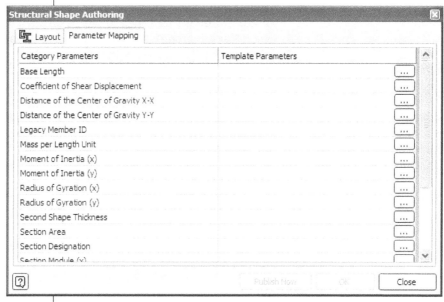

Figure 7–20

Once all the parameters are mapped, you can click **OK** to author
the part. The geometry is automatically revised by the software.
A log file detailing the changes is generated in the working
directory of the part you are authoring.

Step 4 - Publish the structural shape.

Once the structural shape is authored and its design properties set up for documentation, the shape can be published to the Content Center for use in the Frame Generator. To publish, click **Publish Now** in the Structural Shape Authoring dialog box or click ⬚⇨ (Publish Part) in the *Manage* tab>Content Center panel.

Either method opens the Publish Guide dialog box, where you are provided with a series of dialog boxes and are required to click **Next** to progress through the options as you define them. You must select a Library to which to publish, a language, a category, and confirm or edit any properties and parameters. You must then define one or more key columns that uniquely define a family member. For the Family Properties options, you can edit the default values for the Part Number and Description, if required. Select or approve a thumbnail image that is going to be referenced in the Content Center as well as in the Frame Generator. Click **Publish** to publish to the Content Center.

Now that the structural shape has been authored and published, it can be used in your models with the use of Frame Generator.

If the Part Number or Description were previously defined by an expression, it is recommended to edit the value to name the family for publishing.

Practice 7a | Frame Generator

Practice Objectives

- Create an assembly containing a skeletal wireframe.
- Insert frame members into an assembly to create a structural frame assembly, by referencing a skeletal wireframe.
- Reuse inserted frame members where required.
- Adjust frame member ends to obtain the required joints.

In this practice, you will create a simple structural frame assembly to familiarize yourself with using the Frame Generator. You will begin by assembling a part containing the skeletal wireframe into a new assembly. You will then reference the skeletal wireframe to insert the frame members and create the structural frame assembly as shown in Figure 7–21.

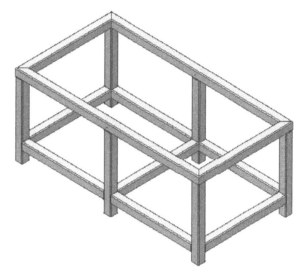

Figure 7–21

3D sketches and solid edges can also be used as references for inserting frame members.

Task 1 - Open a part file.

1. Open **Basic_frame.ipt** from the top-level practice files folder. The part (shown in Figure 7–22), contains the skeletal wireframe that you will reference to create the frame members. It consists of 2D sketches.

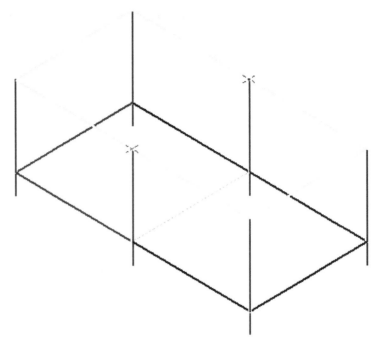

Figure 7–22

2. Close the part file.

Task 2 - Set up the assembly for use with the frame generator.

Once you have the part containing the skeletal wireframe, create a new assembly and place the skeletal wireframe part into the assembly.

1. Create a new assembly file using the metric standard assembly template.

2. Place **Basic_frame.ipt** into the assembly and ground it by right-clicking and selecting **Place Grounded at Origin**. Right-click and select **OK**.

3. Save the assembly as **Structural_Frame.iam** in the top-level practice files folder.

Task 3 - Insert the first frame member.

1. In the *Design* tab>Frame panel, click 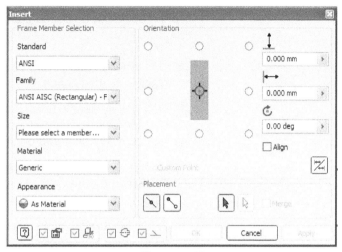 (Insert Frame). The Insert dialog box opens, similar to that shown in Figure 7–23.

Figure 7–23

2. Set the following options for the drop-down lists in the *Frame Member Selection* area:

   - *Standard:* **ANSI**
   - *Family:* **ANSI AISC (Square) - Tube**
   - *Size*: **5x5x1/4**
   - *Material Style:* **Aluminum 6061**
   - *Appearance:* **As Material**

3. In the *Placement* area, click ⬚ to select the members by edge.

4. Select one of the longer edges from **Basic_frame.ipt**. Select in the location shown in Figure 7–24. A preview displays.

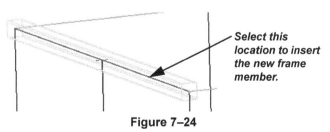

Select this location to insert the new frame member.

Figure 7–24

Hint: Reusing Frame Members

When members are going to be reused, it is recommended that you note the selection location used during the placement of members. The placement location of the parent and the placement location on the entity where the member is being reused define its orientation. Incorrect orientation affects the resulting model when end conditions are added. The orientation can be edited after reuse, if required.

5. In the *Orientation* area, select 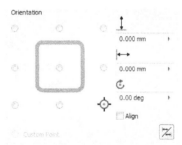, which displays in the middle of the section.

    •   This symbol indicates where the skeletal line reference is with respect to the frame member. The frame member is currently centered on the skeletal line reference.

6. In the *Orientation* area, select the bottom-right button, as shown in Figure 7–25. The frame member preview in the model changes.

    •   The preview might display the skeletal line reference in the bottom-left corner of the frame member, because of the model orientation. Rotate the model to view it from the opposite side and the *Orientation* area in the dialog box then matches the frame member preview in the model.

Figure 7–25

7. Select the center button in the *Orientation* area to return the orientation to its original position. Leave the fields with zero offset and zero angle because offsets or rotation are not required.

8. Verify that ☑ 🖳 (Prompt for File Name) is selected.

9. In the Insert dialog box, click **OK**. The Create New Frame dialog box opens. The frame components are contained in a subassembly, which is created in a subfolder of the directory containing the main assembly.

10. In the Create New Frame dialog box, click **OK**. The Frame Member Naming dialog box opens. A separate part file is created for each frame member that is created. Note that the directory specified under the *File Name* column is the same as the directory specified in the Create New Frame dialog box.

11. In the Frame Member Naming dialog box, click **OK** to accept the default name and path. The first frame member is inserted into the assembly.

Task 4 - Insert additional frame members.

1. Insert a frame member on the entity and in the location shown in Figure 7–26. The settings used in the previous frame member are maintained, use the same options.

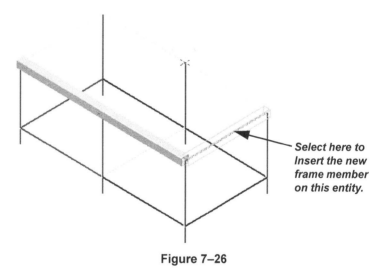

Select here to Insert the new frame member on this entity.

Figure 7–26

2. In the Insert dialog box, click **OK**.

3. Click **OK** to accept the default name and location for the new part file that has been created. Two separate frame members have now been created, as shown in Figure 7–27.

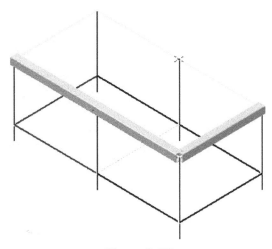

Figure 7–27

4. Insert a frame member on the entity and location shown in Figure 7–28. Ensure that ☑ ⟍ (Select Construction) is selected so the centerline can be selected. In the Insert dialog box, use the previous settings to create the new member.

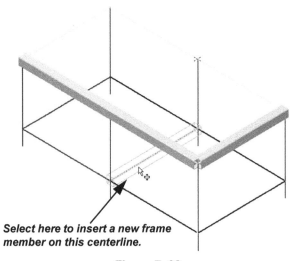

Select here to insert a new frame
member on this centerline.

Figure 7–28

5. In the Insert dialog box, click **OK**.

6. Click **OK** to accept the default name and location for the new part file that has been created. Three separate frame members have now been created, as shown in Figure 7–29.

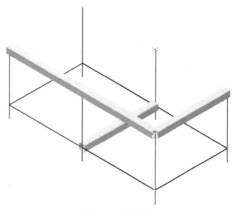

Figure 7–29

Task 5 - Reuse members in the frame.

The three frame members that have been created can be reused to form the remainder of the frame.

1. In the *Design* tab>Frame panel, click (Reuse). The Reuse dialog box opens.

2. Select the first and longest member that was previously created to be reused. Select in the location that was selected when this member was placed. The *Source Member* area in the dialog box updates to display the selected member, as shown in Figure 7–30.

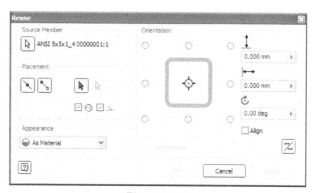

Figure 7–30

3. In the *Placement* area, click ![icon] to select the new entity by edge.

4. Hover the cursor over the remaining entities in the **Basic_Frame.ipt** file. Note that the only selectable entity is the long entity opposite the member that was selected to be reused. This is because it is the only entity in which an identical member can be placed. The lower lines are made up of two line segments, not one long one like the top.

5. Select the entity in the location shown in Figure 7–31. When selecting members to reuse, the selection location on the entity will affect the orientation of the new member. If the orientation is not correct after placement, it can be edited.

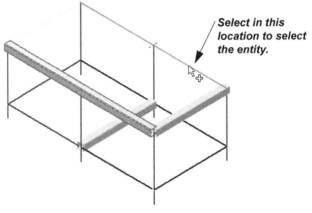

Select in this location to select the entity.

Figure 7–31

6. In the Reuse dialog box, click **OK**. The member displays as shown in Figure 7–32.

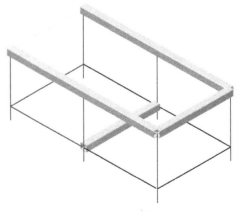

Figure 7–32

7. In the *Design* tab>Frame panel, click ⬚ (Reuse) again.

8. Select the shorter frame member at the top of the frame as the member to be reused. Select in the location that was selected when this member was placed.

9. In the *Placement* area, click ⬚ to select the new entity by edge.

10. Hover the cursor over the remaining frame entities. Note that you can reuse this frame on multiple entities. However, when reusing, note that the end conditions that are assigned to the source member will also be reused. In this case, the top of the frame will be mitered and the bottom will be trimmed and they will not be identical.

11. Select the remaining entity at the top of the frame. Select in the location that was selected on the parent member.

12. In the Reuse dialog box, click **OK**. The member displays as shown in Figure 7–33.

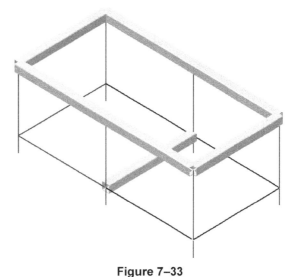

Figure 7–33

Task 6 - Create miter joints.

Once the frame members have been inserted and reused, the frame member ends need to be adjusted to obtain the required joints. This must be done on the source member, not on a reused member.

1. In the *Design* tab>Frame panel, click (Miter). The Miter dialog box opens, as shown in Figure 7–34.

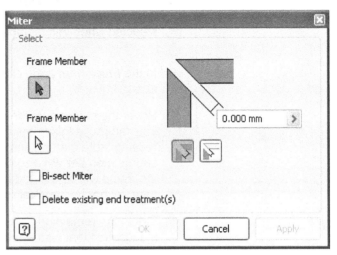

Figure 7–34

2. Confirm that (Miter Cut at both sides) is selected as the miter type.

The order of selection for mitering only matters if you use the miter type .

3. Select the frame members shown in Figure 7–35 as the ones to miter. Note that the reused members are also highlighted, because the miter will also display on these members.

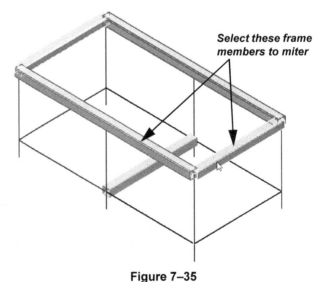

Select these frame members to miter

Figure 7–35

4. Ensure that a value of zero is in the *Miter Cut Extension* field.

5. Click **OK** to apply the miter. The miter displays as shown in Figure 7–36. Note that it also displays on the reused member and that the rotation of the member is currently incorrect. The rotation cannot be controlled by the selection point on the member during placement. The selection point affects the orientation of the member.

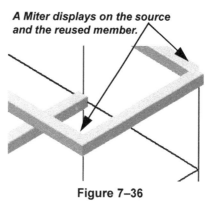

A Miter displays on the source and the reused member.

Figure 7–36

6. In the *Design* tab>Frame panel, click 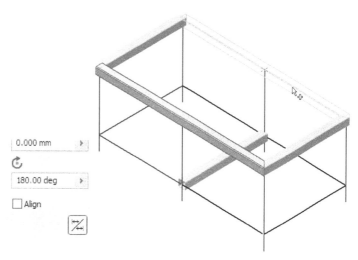 (Change Reuse). The Change Reuse dialog box opens. Select the reused member shown in Figure 7–37. In the *Orientation* area, in the *Rotation* field, enter **180.00 deg**.

0.000 mm

180.00 deg

Align

Figure 7–37

7. Click **OK** to update the change in the model.

8. Review the orientation of the miter that was added to the reused shorter member. Since a miter will be added to both ends, an incorrect orientation is not an issue. The rotation of the member will be adjusted after mitering the other end.

9. In the *Design* tab>Frame panel, click ⌐ (Miter). The Miter dialog box opens, Select the members in Figure 7–38 to miter.

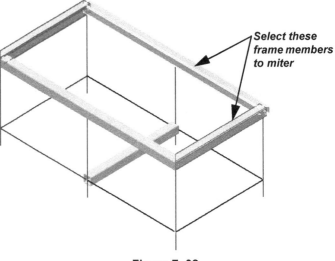

Select these
frame members
to miter

Figure 7–38

10. Ensure that a value of **0** displays in the *Miter Cut Extension* field.

11. Click **OK** to apply the miter.

12. In the *Design* tab>Frame panel, click ⟋ (Change Reuse). The Change Reuse dialog box opens. Select the reused member shown in Figure 7–39. In the *Orientation* area, in the *Rotation* field, enter **180.00 deg**,

Figure 7–39

13. Click **OK** to update the change in the model.

14. Miter the remaining corner to complete the top of the frame, as shown in Figure 7–40.

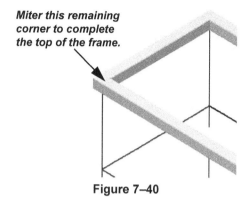

Miter this remaining corner to complete the top of the frame.

Figure 7–40

Task 7 - Insert a new frame member and reuse members to complete the assembly.

---

1. Click 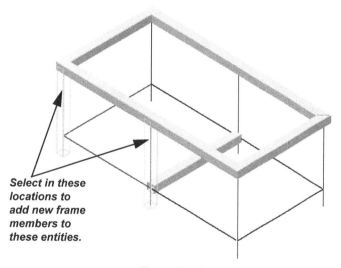 (Insert Frame). The Insert dialog box opens. Maintain the same member settings and locate two new members on the entities shown in Figure 7–41. Two unique members are required because of the end conditions. Select near the top of both entities to locate the new members.

Select in these locations to add new frame members to these entities.

Figure 7–41

2. Click ⲦⲦ (Reuse).

3. Select the corner frame member and reuse it to create the frame shown in Figure 7–42. Select near the top of all of the corner entities to place the reused members. Click **Apply** to finalize the members while remaining in the Reuse dialog box.

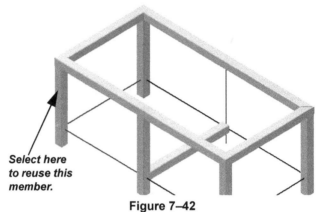

Select here
to reuse this
member.

Figure 7–42

4. In the Reuse dialog box, in the *Source Member* area, click

   ⬚ and select the center vertical member. Select the one remaining vertical entity (near the top) to place it. Click **Apply**. The assembly displays as shown in Figure 7–43.

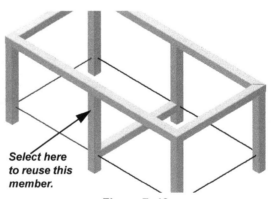

Select here
to reuse this
member.

Figure 7–43

5. In the Reuse dialog box, click ⬚ and select the member that was created on the centerline in the location shown in Figure 7–44.

6. Select the remaining six entities (shown highlighted in Figure 7–44). This member will be reused on all of these entities.

Select here to reuse
this member.

Figure 7–44

7. In the Reuse dialog box, click **OK**.

8. Save the assembly and all of the required components.

Task 8 - Use the Trim To Frame option.

1. In the *Design* tab>Frame panel, click ⏚ (Trim to Frame). The Trim to Frame dialog box opens, as shown in Figure 7–45.

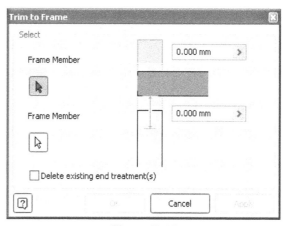

Figure 7–45

The reused members also highlight because the trim will also be applied to them.

2. Select the first frame member (blue reference), shown in Figure 7–46.

3. Select the second frame member (yellow reference) shown in Figure 7–46. The first frame member is trimmed to the second intersecting face of the second frame member. The second frame member is trimmed or extended to the first intersecting face of the first frame member.

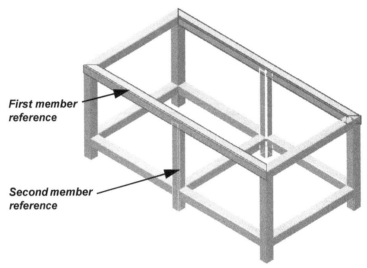

First member reference

Second member reference

Figure 7–46

4. Leave the vertical and horizontal offset values for trimming as **0** and click **OK**.

5. The Frame Generator dialog box opens. Note that the error message prompts you that the miter that you applied earlier cannot be calculated because the frame member is now too short. Click **OK**.

6. The trimmed members are shown in Figure 7–47. The **Trim To Frame** option trims both parent members.

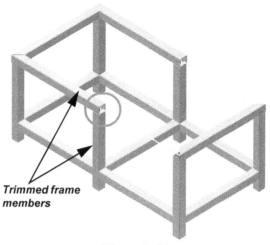

Trimmed frame members

Figure 7–47

7. The result is not correct. To restore the frame members to their original state, when they were created (i.e., before trims, extensions, lengthens, notches, and miters.), in the *Design* tab>expanded Frame panel, click ✂ (Remove End Treatments).

8. Select the two trimmed members resulting from the **Trim to Frame** option, and click **OK**. The assembly should return to the state shown in Figure 7–48. Note that the trim and the miters are undone.

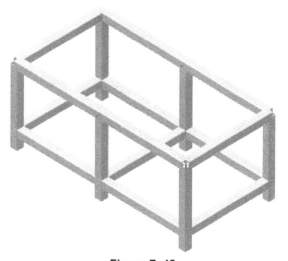

Figure 7–48

9. Because you want to keep the miters that you added before the trim, in the Quick Access Toolbar, click 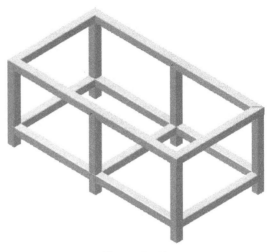 (Undo) twice to return to the assembly shown in Figure 7–49. The miters are intact, but the trim is undone. In this case, **Undo** works because the trim was performed during the same session of the software. If the assembly was opened in a separate session of the software, it would not be possible to use the **Undo** option.

Figure 7–49

Task 9 - Use the Trim/Extend option.

1. In the *Design* tab>Frame panel, click ^{°|⊩} (Trim/Extend). The Trim - Extend To Face dialog box opens, as shown in Figure 7–50.

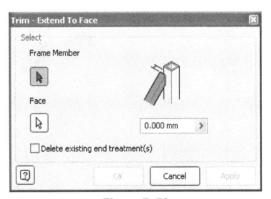

Figure 7–50

2. Select the two parent vertical frame members shown in Figure 7–51 to trim to a common face.

3. Click 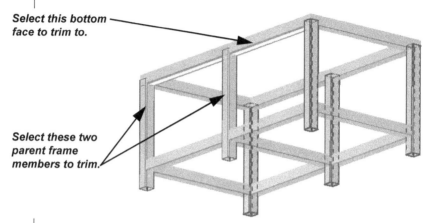 (Select face to cut or lengthen) under *Face*, and select the face shown in Figure 7–51 to which the selected frame members will be trimmed.

Select this bottom face to trim to.

Select these two parent frame members to trim.

Figure 7–51

4. Leave an offset value of **0**.

5. Click **OK** to trim the frame member(s). The two parent frame members and the reused members also update.

6. Change the view display to **Shaded with Edges**. This will help you to identify whether the entities were trimmed correctly. Review the locations in which each member comes into contact with the top frame members. Is there any overlap similar to that shown in Figure 7–52?

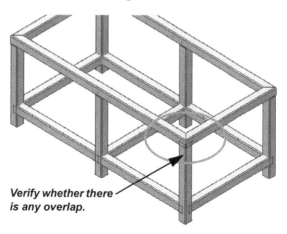

Verify whether there is any overlap.

Figure 7–52

7. The overlap on the frame members is not because the reused member did not update, it is because it was oriented differently when it is placed based on where the entity was selected. If any of the members are incorrectly oriented, open the Change Reuse dialog box, select a reused member that is not oriented correctly, and in the *Select* area, click

🖻 (Reverse Member Direction) and then click **Apply**. This reversal is only required if the placement location varies from the original selection location on the member being reused. Repeat and reverse the direction on any other members, as required. The assembly displays as shown in Figure 7–53.

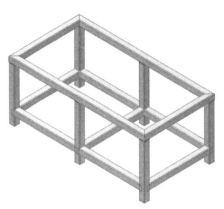

Figure 7–53

8. Use ⸱ǁᖴ (Trim/Extend) again to trim the remaining parent member. You will need to trim it on both ends. The completed frame assembly is shown in Figure 7–54.

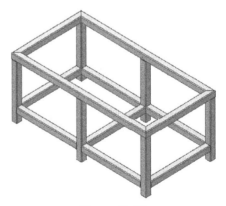

Figure 7–54

9. Save the assembly and all of its components. Close the window.

Chapter Review Questions

1. Which of the following entities can be selected in the skeletal wireframe model to define the location of structural frame members? (Select all that apply.)

    a. Lines in a 2D sketch

    b. Lines in a 3D sketch

    c. Points

    d. Centerlines

    e. Construction Lines

    f. Splines

2. How do you access the **Frame Generator** options?

    a. *Assemble* tab>Frame panel

    b. *Environments* tab>Frame panel

    c. *Design* tab>Frame panel

    d. *Design* tab>Fasten panel

3. What does the *Orientation* area (shown in Figure 7–55), enable you to do when inserting a member?

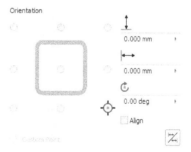

Figure 7–55

    a. Locate the position of the profile with respect to the reference.

    b. Define the end treatments available to the frame member.

    c. Define the shape of the profile for the frame member.

    d. All of the above.

4. Which of the following are true statements about reusing frame generated members? (Select all that apply.)

    a. The **Reuse** command enables you to reuse members that were generated in other assembly files.

    b. The direction in which a reused member is inserted along a new entity depends on where on the entity the reference is selected.

    c. To rotate a reused member about the reference entity,

       click (Reverse Member Direction).

    d. End conditions, such as Miters created on a parent member, reflect in all of the reused members.

5. The **Change Reuse** option enables you to edit a reused member's orientation.

    a. True

    b. False

6. Which of the following Miter types should be used to miter with a gap on the first selected frame member equal to the defined value?

    a.

    b.

7. Which of the following Frame options does not enable you to modify the joints between members?

    a. **Notch**

    b. **Miter**

    c. **Lengthen/Shorten**

    d. **Trim To Frame**

8. What is the purpose of the Structural Shape Author?

    a. Publish a frame assembly for use in other projects.

    b. Automatically create a structural shape frame.

    c. Define new styles of end treatments, such as miters.

    d. Publish user-defined custom profiles to a library.

Answers: 1.(a,b,c,d,e,f), 2.c, 3.a, 4.(b,d), 5.a, 6.b, 7.c, 8.d

Command Summary

Button	Command	Location
	Beam/ Column Calculator	• **Ribbon:** *Design* tab>expanded Frame panel
	Change	• **Ribbon:** *Design* tab>Frame panel
	Change Reuse	• **Ribbon:** *Design* tab>Frame panel
	Frame Member Info	• **Ribbon:** *Design* tab>expanded Frame panel
	Insert Frame	• **Ribbon:** *Design* tab>Frame panel
	Lengthen/ Shorten	• **Ribbon:** *Design* tab>Frame panel
	Miter	• **Ribbon:** *Design* tab>Frame panel
	Notch	• **Ribbon:** *Design* tab>Frame panel
	Plate Calculator	• **Ribbon:** *Design* tab>expanded Frame panel
	Publish Part	• **Ribbon**: *Manage* tab>Content Center panel
	Remove End Treatments	• **Ribbon:** *Design* tab>expanded Frame panel
	Reuse	• **Ribbon:** *Design* tab>Frame panel
	Structural Shape Authoring	• **Ribbon:** *Manage* tab>Author panel
	Trim/Extend	• **Ribbon:** *Design* tab>Frame panel
	Trim to Frame	• **Ribbon:** *Design* tab>Frame panel

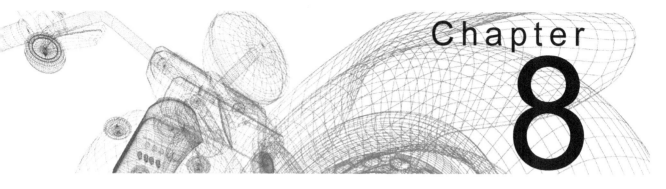

Design Accelerator

The Design Accelerator enables you to easily insert standard and customized components and features into your model. The Design Accelerator also contains engineering calculators that are used to verify your designs, as well as the Engineer's Handbooks, which is a reference tool for engineering formulas used by the calculators.

Learning Objectives in this Chapter

- Automatically create geometry using component generators.
- Understand what kind of calculations to perform to help assess the feasibility of designs based on provided data.
- Access the Engineer's Handbook as a reference for theories and formulas while using the generators and calculators.

8.1 Design Accelerator

The Design Accelerator tools enable you to generate common components and perform calculations for them by entering mechanical attributes. The tools include generators, calculators, and the Engineer's Handbook, which are all found on the *Design* tab. The commands in the *Design* tab are shown in Figure 8–1 with all of the panel flyouts pinned open.

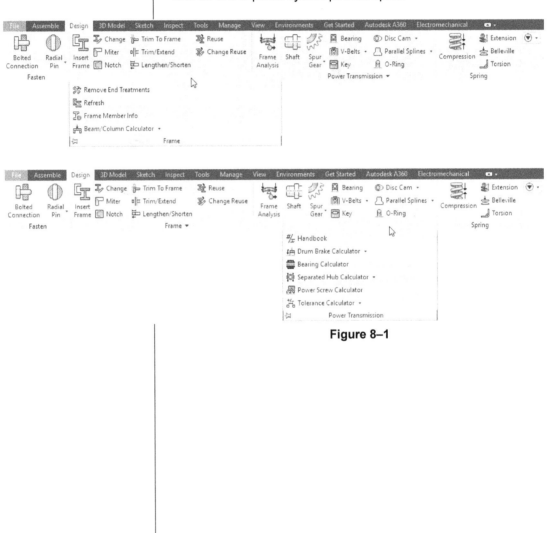

Figure 8–1

8.2 Generators

Generators use specific mechanical attributes and dimensions to automatically create components. For example, a clevis pin can be created automatically with the Design Accelerator by specifying the clevis width, rod width, pin diameter, and active pin length. Generators enable you to focus on the function of your design and enable the geometry to be created for you.

General Steps

Use the following general steps to insert a component using the Design Accelerator's Generator tools:

1. Select the required component generator.
2. Enter and select the required inputs.
3. Perform calculations, as required.
4. Correct errors, as required.
5. Complete the generator.

Step 1 - Select the required component generator.

Select the required component generator from the *Design* tab of the ribbon. They are grouped in panels according to functional areas. The interface for each of the generators is a single dialog box containing a *Design* tab to define the component parameters and a *Calculation* tab to verify the design. Using the *Calculation* tab is optional, but using it helps to make your designs more robust by verifying that your components meet design requirements. Some component generators have tabs for additional calculations or graphs.

The Spur Gears Component Generator is shown as an example in Figure 8–2. In the *Design* tab, you input required data to create the components and select references to place the components.

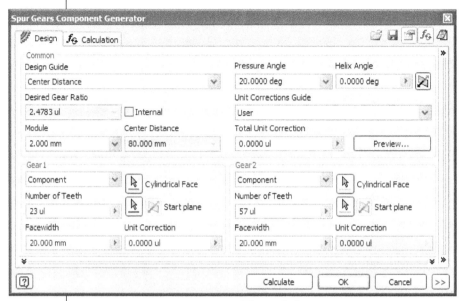

Figure 8–2

Another dialog box style interface exists for particular generators, such as bolted connections and clevis pins. These dialog boxes contain a built-in link to the Content Center that enables you to add several standard components, such as bolts, washers, and nuts, to the base component. The bolted connections dialog box is shown in Figure 8–3. Some common areas are labeled.

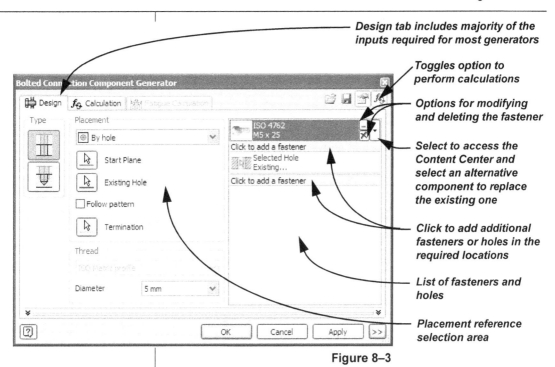

Design tab includes majority of the inputs required for most generators

Toggles option to perform calculations

Options for modifying and deleting the fastener

Select to access the Content Center and select an alternative component to replace the existing one

Click to add additional fasteners or holes in the required locations

List of fasteners and holes

Placement reference selection area

Figure 8–3

Each generator contains only the fields and options applicable to that generator.

Step 2 - Enter and select the required inputs.

For some component generator dialog boxes, you can immediately select the placement references, such as for bolted connections, key connections, and spur gears. Select the required references, as required. Enter and select the required inputs, as required, such as a thread and diameter value.

*Depending on the components added, you might be able to add fasteners at different locations. This is possible when you see multiple **Click to add a fastener** options.*

Some component generator dialog boxes enable you to select components from the Content Center, such as for bolted connections, bearings, and clevis pins. For example, to add a fastener in the Bolted Connection Component Generator, click **Click to add a fastener** in the list of fasteners and holes, as shown in Figure 8–3, and select the required fastener from the Content Center. Continue adding fasteners and holes as required.

Step 3 - Perform calculations, as required.

To perform calculations to determine if components are able to withstand particular forces and loads, use the options in the *Calculation* tab. Select the type of calculation, input the required loads, and select materials in the *Calculation* tab. The *Calculation* tab for each generator is different, the common areas are labeled in Figure 8–4.

Expandable   **Loads**   **Expandable**   **Icons**   **Expansion and**
calculations report area   **input area**   **results area**   **Compression arrows**

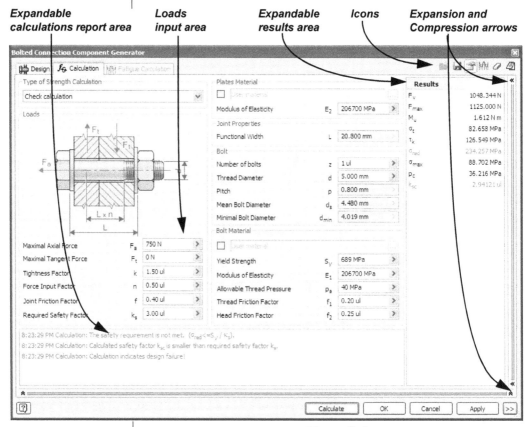

Figure 8–4

To perform calculations, enter the required data and click **Calculate**.

- The results display in the expandable results area on the right side. View a report for the calculations by expanding the bottom area. This area indicates if the calculations show design compliance or design failure based on the values entered. To expand or collapse the expandable areas, select the expansion and compression arrows. To change the units of any value in the results area, double-click on the value and enter the new units.

- When the input values cause a design failure, the critical values that have been exceeded are highlighted in red in the Results area. The calculations report displays information about the results. Blue text signifies general information about the calculation, while red text describes failed results. Text with a red background means there is a critical error and you cannot continue the design unless you change inputs.

Step 4 - Correct errors, as required.

You can place components that fail the calculation checks but it is typically required to resolve the errors. You can resolve the errors by changing the forces, material, or other information on the *Calculation* tab, or you can change the parameters on the *Design* tab. After the information is modified, click **Calculate** to perform the calculation with the new information.

Step 5 - Complete the generator.

Once you have completed defining the component, click **OK** to place the component.

8.3 Calculators

Calculators in the Design Accelerator perform calculations to help assess the feasibility of designs based on provided data. The Plate Calculator dialog box is shown in Figure 8–5. The calculators are similar to the *Calculation* tab for generators, except they do not generate geometry. For example, use the plate calculator to enter the beam dimensions, load, and material properties to determine if a rectangular beam can withstand a load. If the beam's properties are sufficient, a calculated safety factor is provided.

To access the calculators, you might have to expand the panels on the Design tab to access their commands.

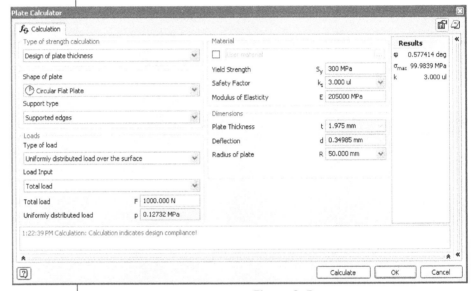

Figure 8–5

The list of calculators available include the following:

*The calculators listed with the * symbol adjacent to their names are located on the Environments tab in the Convert panel. They deal with weldments.*

• **Band Brake**	• **Disc Brake**	• **Power Screw**
• **Beam and Column**	• **Drum Brake**	• **Press Fit**
• **Bevel Solder***	• **Fillet Weld (Plane)***	• **Separated Hub**
• **Butt Solder***	• **Fillet Weld (Spatial)***	• **Slotted Hub**
• **Butt Weld ***	• **Lap Solder***	• **Spot Weld ***
• **Bearing**	• **Limits and Fits**	• **Step Solder***
• **Cone Brake**	• **Plate**	• **Step Tube Solder***
• **Cone Joint**	• **Plug and Groove Weld ***	• **Tolerance**

8.4 Engineer's Handbook

The Engineer's Handbook is a reference for all theories and formulas used in the generators and calculators. To open the Handbook, click $\#/x$ (Handbook) in the expanded Power Transmission panel on the *Design* tab. A sample of the Engineer's Handbook is shown in Figure 8–6.

- If the online Help document does not automatically open the Engineer's Handbook. In the Search field, type **Engineer's Handbook** to view the information.

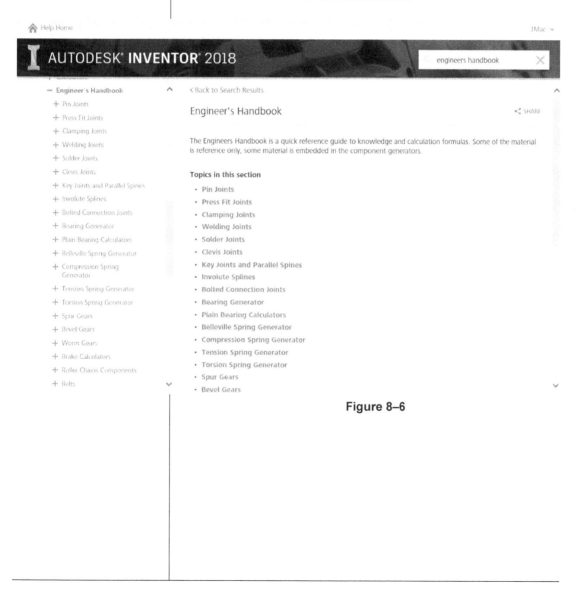

Figure 8–6

Practice 8a

Design Accelerator I

Practice Objective

- Automatically insert a component using the **Radial Pin** component generator and the Content Center.

In this practice, you insert a pin using the Radial Pin component generator and Content Center. The final assembly is shown in Figure 8–7.

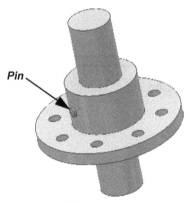

Pin

Figure 8–7

Task 1 - Use the radial pin component generator.

1. Open **hub_shaft_assy.iam** from the top level practice files folder. The model displays as shown in Figure 8–8.

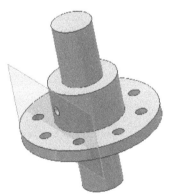

Figure 8–8

Hint: Accessing Content Center data through Vault.

If you do not have Desktop Content installed on your local system and use Vault, you must log in to access the Content Center data, otherwise go to Step 2 to complete the practice. To log in, click **File>Vault Server>Log In**. If the **Log In** option is grayed out, then you are already logged in and you can proceed to the next step. Otherwise, click

Log In
Enables secure access to the server. , activate the **Content Center library read only user** option in the Authentication drop-down list and click **OK**. The **Content Center library read only user** option enables you to log in with read only permissions if you do not have a login set up with your system administrator. You are now logged into the Content Center.

2. In the ribbon, select the *Design* tab to access the Design Accelerator tools.

3. In the *Design* tab>Fasten panel, click 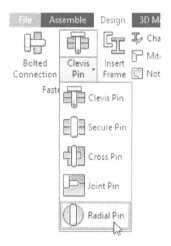 (Radial Pin). You might need to select it from the pin flyout menu, as shown in Figure 8–9. The Radial Pin Component Generator dialog box opens.

Figure 8–9

4. Select the visible work plane as the start plane.

5. Select the hole shown in Figure 8–10. The selected hole is added to the Items list in the dialog box.

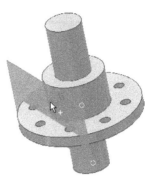

Figure 8–10

6. Select **Click to add a pin** from the Items list. The fasteners available in the Content Center display.

7. Select **ISO 8734 A** from the list. A preview of the pin displays.

   If the direction of the pin is incorrect, reverse it using 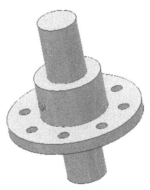 for the Existing Hole. Note how the length of the pin is automatically selected, based on the length of the existing hole.

8. Click **OK** to insert the pin into the assembly. If the File Naming dialog box displays, click **OK** to accept the default name.

9. Toggle off the visibility of **Work Plane2**. The assembly displays as shown in Figure 8–11.

Figure 8–11

10. Save and close the assembly.

Practice 8b

Design Accelerator II

Practice Objective

* Place a set of fasteners from the Content Center and create a hole through a part, using the **Bolted Connection** component generator, all in individual tasks, and then all in a single task.

In this practice, you use the Content Center and Design Accelerator to insert a screw, washer, and nut into the four holes shown in Figure 8–12. During the placement of one set of fasteners, you also create a hole through one of the parts using the bolted connection component generator. By placing components using both methods, you can determine which one is the faster method for placing bolted connections.

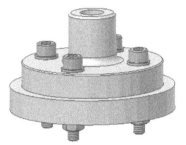

Figure 8–12

Task 1 - Place a washer from the Content Center.

In this task, you assemble components directly from the Content Center into the assembly. In a later task you will use the Design Accelerator to assemble the same components and you can compare the process for each.

1. Open **general.iam** from the *Design_Accelerator2* folder. The assembly displays as shown in Figure 8–13.

Figure 8–13

2. Rotate the model to the opposite side and note that the plate has only three identical holes, as shown in Figure 8–14, but four identical holes on the flange.

Figure 8–14

*The **Content Center** **library read only user** option enables you to log in with read only permissions if you do not have a login set up with your system administrator.*

3. In the *Assemble* tab>Component panel, click  (Place from Content Center). If the Log In dialog box opens, activate the **Content Center library read only user** option and click **OK** to open the Content Center dialog box.

4. Toggle on (AutoDrop) if it is not already on.

5. Toggle on the Tree and Table View panes using and , if they are not already displayed. The Content Center is shown in Figure 8–15. You can also change the display of the items. In Figure 8–15 the items display as thumbnails.

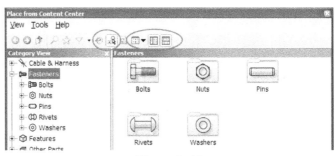

Figure 8–15

6. Expand the *Fasteners* category and then expand the *Washers* category in the Category View pane.

7. Select the *Plain* category and select **ISO 7089**. The Table View pane should display as shown in Figure 8–16. If not, select the preview border and drag it upwards.

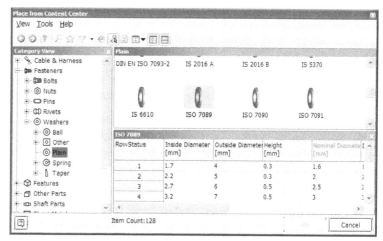

Figure 8–16

8. Double-click on **ISO 7089** in the upper pane.

9. Place the cursor on the edge of one of the holes on the flange that corresponds with one of the holes on the plate. Recall that only three holes are on the plate. Do not select the hole at the center of the part.

You can also insert bolted connections based on points, 3D points, and work points created in the sketch environment.

10. Click to accept the previewed washer and click ⬚ to complete the washer placement. ⬚ is enabled by default, which sets the Autodesk Inventor software to assemble the Content Center item to all members in a pattern or, in this case, all sketched points dealing with the selected feature, as shown in Figure 8–17.

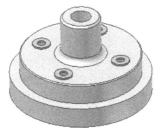

Figure 8–17

11. Delete the three washers from the assembly that were automatically added.

Task 2 - Place a screw from the Content Center.

In this task, you use an alternative method of accessing the Content Center to place a screw.

1. In the Model Browser drop-down list, select **Favorites**, as shown in Figure 8–18. The Favorites browser shows the Content Center categories.

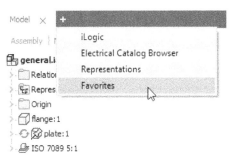

Figure 8–18

2. Expand the following categories in order: Fasteners, Bolts, and Socket Head. Double-click on **ISO 4762** to place it.

3. Place the cursor over the inner edge of the washer. Left-click the preview to accept it. A directional arrow displays. Drag it to increase the length of the screw so that it goes through the length of both holes and protrudes out, as shown in Figure 8–19. The bolt should be an M5 x 30.

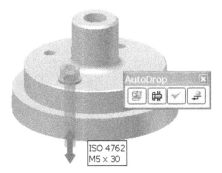

Figure 8–19

Note that ⬚ is not available in the **AutoDrop** menu. This is because there is no pattern to follow. If there were multiple bolts to add, you would need to add them manually using this method.

4. Click ⬚ to complete the bolt placement.

Task 3 - Place a nut from the Content Center.

1. Place an **ISO 4032** hex nut, using either of the methods used previously. Because you are placing the nut by referencing the edge of the hole, the software recognizes that the edge belongs to a sketch and the entire set of holes are selected.

   Click 🔲 in the AutoDrop dialog box to disable this pattern/sketch functionality. The model (with a single nut) should display as shown in Figure 8–20. Click 🔲.

Figure 8–20

2. Select **Modeling** at the top of the Model Browser and review the **Flange.ipt** model to see that the holes were created referencing a sketch that consisted of points. **Plate.ipt** referenced the holes in the flange for their creation.

Task 4 - Insert one set of fasteners using the Design Accelerator.

In this task, you use an alternative method of placing fasteners. This involves using the bolted connection component generator.

1. Select the *Design* tab. The ribbon displays as shown in Figure 8–21, listing all of the Design Accelerator tools (generators, calculators, and the Engineer's Handbook).

Figure 8–21

2. In the *Design* tab>Fasten panel, click 🔲 (Bolted Connection) to open the Bolted Connection Component Generator.

3. Keep the hole type as 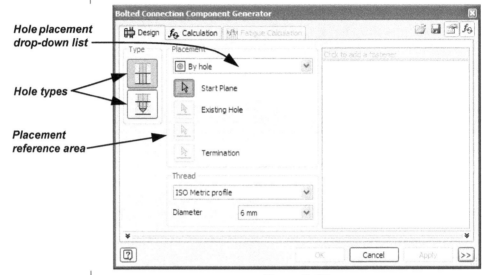 (Through All connection type).

4. Set the hole placement drop-down list to **By hole**. The Bolted Connection Component Generator dialog box displays as shown in Figure 8–22.

Hole placement drop-down list

Hole types

Placement reference area

Figure 8–22

5. Select the references shown in Figure 8–23. Ensure that the hole you select has a matching hole in the plate.

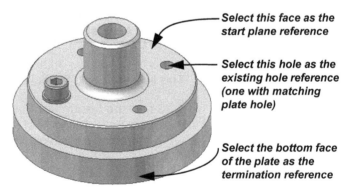

Select this face as the start plane reference

Select this hole as the existing hole reference (one with matching plate hole)

Select the bottom face of the plate as the termination reference

Figure 8–23

6. Set the *Thread* parameters to **ISO Metric profile** and the *Diameter* to **5mm**.

7. Click **Click to add a fastener** to access the bolt in the Content Center. Set *Standard* to **<All>** and *Category* to **Socket Head Bolts**, as shown in Figure 8–24.

Figure 8–24

8. Select **ISO 4762**. A preview of the screw displays in the model and is placed in the list in the dialog box, as shown in Figure 8–25.

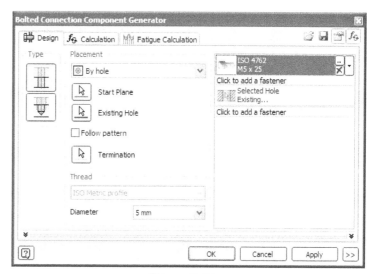

Figure 8–25

9. Click **Click to add a fastener** that is just below the screw in the list to place a washer between the screw and the hole.

10. Select the **ISO 7089** washer. The washer displays as shown in Figure 8–26. Note the length of the screw in the preview.

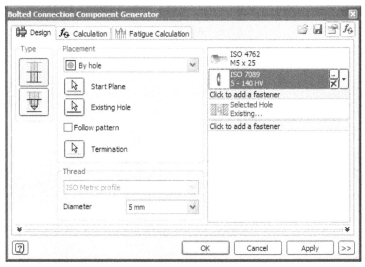

Figure 8–26

11. Click **Click to add a fastener** that is below the hole in the list to place a nut after it. Select **Nuts** from the *Category* drop-down list.

12. Select the **ISO 4032** hex nut. The list displays as shown in Figure 8–27. Note the length of the screw increased in length after the nut was added.

Figure 8–27

13. Click **OK** to complete the placement of the bolted connection. If the File Naming dialog box displays, click **OK** to accept the default name. The model now displays as shown in Figure 8–28.

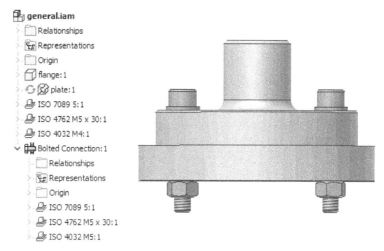

general.iam
  > Relationships
  > Representations
  > Origin
  > flange:1
  > plate:1
  > ISO 7089 5:1
  > ISO 4762 M5 x 30:1
  > ISO 4032 M4:1
  ∨ Bolted Connection:1
      Relationships
    > Representations
    > Origin
    > ISO 7089 5:1
    > ISO 4762 M5 x 30:1
    > ISO 4032 M5:1

Figure 8–28

Task 5 - Edit the bolted connection and save to the Templates Library.

You will use the same components multiple times throughout this task. If you have a set of fasteners that you use often, you can save that grouping to the Bolted Connection Templates Library for later use. This saves considerable time selecting components and ensures you use the same grouping each time.

1. In the Model Browser, right-click on **Bolted Connection:1** and select **Edit using Design Accelerator**. The Bolted Connection Component Generator displays.

2. Click ⟩⟩ to expand the dialog box if it is not already expanded.

3. Click **Add...** in the Templates Library area to add the component grouping to the library. The Template Description dialog box displays.

4. Click **OK** to accept the default name. If the name already exists, enter a unique name or delete the existing template.

5. Click **Cancel** to close the dialog box.

Task 6 - Use Design Accelerator to simultaneously insert fasteners and create a hole in the plate.

If you need to insert fasteners but a hole does not exist in one or more of the parts, the Bolted Connection component generator can create the hole for you in the same dialog box.

1. In the *Design* tab>Fasten panel, click ⬚ (Bolted Connection) to open the Bolted Connection Component Generator.

2. Select the same start plane you used for the last bolted connection (the top face of the flange).

3. For the Existing Hole reference, select the hole in the flange that does not have a corresponding hole in the plate.

4. Select the bottom face of the plate for the Termination reference, as shown in Figure 8–29. A new hole is previewed in the plate because of the Termination reference you selected. The list of holes and fasteners now shows two holes instead of just one.

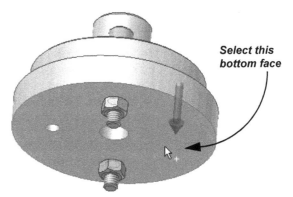

Select this bottom face

Figure 8–29

5. Click ⬚ to expand the dialog box if it is not already expanded.

6. Select the template you created earlier (**ISO 4762 M5 x 30** by default) and click **SET**. This loads the grouping of components.

7. Click **OK** to insert the bolted connection. If the File Naming dialog box displays, click **OK** to accept the default name. The assembly displays as shown in Figure 8–30.

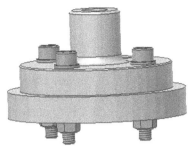

Figure 8–30

Task 7 - Place the fasteners for the last pair of holes.

1. Place the fasteners for the last hole in the flange. You can use ▨ (Place from Content Center) in the *Assemble* tab, or use ▨ (Bolted Connection) in the *Design* tab.

Task 8 - Delete all fasteners and place using the Follow Pattern option.

1. Delete all of the fasteners in the assembly.

2. In the *Design* tab, click ▨ (Bolted Connection) and select the same start plane as you previously selected. Select an existing Hole reference, and select the bottom face of the plate as the Termination reference.

3. As soon as you select a hole, the dialog box updates and adds the **Follow pattern** option. Select this option to enable it.

4. Select the **ISO 4762 M5x30** template, click **SET**. Click **OK** twice to complete the command and accept the default names. All fasteners should now be added to the assembly. The fasteners are placed on all of the holes. This is an excellent method for fast placement of similar fasteners. Consider using patterns and sketches when placing holes in your models that will later be populated with fasteners.

Task 9 - Modify the thickness on the flange component.

1. Open **flange.ipt**. Change the thickness value of **Extrusion1** from *10mm* to **20 mm**.

2. Return to the assembly and update the model. Note that the bolt length is now too short and the nuts are consumed in the plate component. At this point, you can right-click on the bolted connection and select **Edit using Design Accelerator** to open the Bolted Connection Component Generator. Click **OK** to close the dialog box. The size of the bolts updates immediately.

3. Save and close all models.

> **Hint: Automatic Solve**
>
> The **Automatic Solve** option automatically updates all generated components when a change is made in an assembly component. By default, this option is toggled off, requiring the manual update. To enable, right-click on **Bolted Connection** in the assembly and select **Component>Automatic Solve**.
>
> displays next to the **Bolted Connection** node in the Model Browser, indicating that it now automatically updates if changes are made.

Chapter Review Questions

1. What is the purpose of the Design Accelerator?

    a. To generate geometry and perform calculations for common components.

    b. To use LOD Representations to speed up the loading of assemblies.

    c. To minimize hardware resources.

    d. To speed up drawing tasks in a Sketch.

2. The Content Center is automatically accessed in a Generator.

    a. True

    b. False

3. Which tool can you use to understand the theory used in Generators and calculators?

    a. Bolted Connection

    b. Frame Generator

    c. Engineer's Handbook

    d. Various Calculators

4. If the generator fails to generate a component that cuts through solid material, you must modify the geometry appropriately and rerun the generator.

    a. True

    b. False

Command Summary

Button	Command	Location
NA	Fasteners	• **Ribbon**: *Design* tab>Fasten panel
NA	Frame Commands	• **Ribbon**: *Design* tab>Frame panel
$\#/x$	Handbook	• **Ribbon**: ***Design*** tab>expanded Power Transmission panel
NA	Power Transmission Commands	• **Ribbon**: *Design* tab>Power Transmission panel
NA	Springs	• **Ribbon**: *Design* tab>Spring panel

Index

T

www.ingramcontent.com/pod-product-compliance
Lightning Source LLC
Chambersburg PA
CBHW080404060326
40689CB00019B/4126